CHOICES II

What is The Future of Life on This beautiful Plan-E.T. - will WE LIVE or DIE?

Published 2020: Golden Child Promotions Publishing Ltd

Portland House,
Belmont Business Park,
Durham,
DH1 1TW

9x9x9@goldenchildpromotionspublishing.com

Copyright © 2020 by Kwadw(o) Naya: Baa Ankh Em Ra A'lyun Eil. All rights reserved. No part of this publication may be reproduced, stored in a retrieval system or transmitted in any form or by any means, electronic, mechanical, photocopying, recording, and/or otherwise without prior written permission of the publishers. This book may not be lent, resold, hired out or otherwise disposed of by way of trade in any form, binding or cover other than that in which it is published, without the prior consent of the publishers.

LIFEandDEATH
ANKHandCROSS

"To progress spiritually one must be at peace, not disturbed by commitments or life. Therefore, it is important to pay bills and people on time and maintain happy relationships with others!"
— Kwadw(o) Naya: Baa Ankh Em Ra A'lyun Eil

READ THIS FIRST

DOWNLOAD CHOICES 1 EBOOK FREE

I would like to give you Choices 1 free just in case you have not had a chance to read it.

https://bookhip.com/FJVSKH

DEDICATION

I would like to dedicate this to all truth seekers especially the ones that are spiritually awake. As now is a time where we need to sort the living out from the dead.

ACKNOWLEDGEMENTS

I would like to give a big thanks to Eben Chidike, hansbarrow, SMFweb Designs, Hayley Jukes, João Cabral from Pexels for the book cover background image, and Victoria Corrie.

This book would never have been published without the assistance of these wonderful individuals.

Thank you once again.

PREFACE

"Those who know better should do better."
– Patricia Franklin

Hi, I hope you are all well!

I guess we are back once again for another installment. I hope you enjoyed the last book; this one is pretty much a follow on.

It is exciting times at the moment, changing times. Soon everyone's **perception** of the world as they know it will change, mark my words and that will be before the year 2038. These are my words and I am happy to stand by them.

As said previously, when I look around the world, nothing makes sense anymore, not to me anyway. We taxpayers (**general consumers**) relate more to **technology** than **nature**, we seem to lean more towards quick unnatural fast food and products opposed to the natural. If you rewind the clock sixty years to the time of our foremothers and fathers, things were totally different. They were all living a more natural and healthy life.

Would you agree?

CONTENTS

Dedication xi
Acknowledgements xii
Preface xiii
Chapter 1: New Times 1
Chapter 2: Monopolies 9
    What Is Monopoly? 10
        What Is The Fortune 500? 11
        The Basics Of The Fortune 500 11
        Fortune 500 2018 12
Chapter 3: Mind Control 21
Chapter 4: From A.I. To A.G.I. 28
    What Is AI? 30
    But What About AGI? 31
Chapter 5: Cognitive Dissonance 39
Chapter 6: L.G.B.T.Q. Agendas 45
    List Of Genders 56

Chapter 7A: UFOs, IFOs, And OOTWFOs 58
    Has Anyone Seen A UFO? 63
    Now Let Us Get On To IFOs. 70
    Is This An OOTWFO? 80
    What Is Life? 91
    Your Time Is Over And You Know It! 96
Chapter 7B: Disclosure 99
Chapter 8: Freedom, Happiness, And Consciousness 131
    What Comes Next? Choices! 132
    What Is Your Purpose For This Life? 133
Chapter 9: Responsibility, Freedom, And Creative Power 138
    Why Is This So? 139
    What Is Going On? 140
Conclusion 152
About The Author 157

CHAPTER 1
NEW TIMES

Over the next ten to twenty years WE are ALL going to be SEEING and EXPERIENCING a lot of CHANGES. It is going to BE THE END OF THE WORLD as WE KNOW it. The END of US if WE don't FIX UP. But that CHOICE is down to US.

These TIMES, the TIMES of the SEVEN THUNDERS which are upon US were prophesized over two thousand years ago. Have you heard of the Seven Thunders? They are highlighted in The Holy Bible and the Holy Tablets:

> **Revelation 10:3-4**
>
> *"And cried with a loud voice, as when a lion roareth: and when he had cried, seven thunders uttered their voices. And when the seven thunders had uttered their voices, I was about to write: and I heard a voice from heaven saying unto me, Seal up those things which the seven thunders uttered, and write them not."*[1]
>
> If you read the full chapter, it goes into it in much more detail, but it is hard to decipher from the bible the true meaning due to the way it has been translated. The Holy Tablets are much clearer and precise.
>
> Take a look at the following extract from The Holy Tablets concerning the Seven Thunders so you can see for yourself:

---

[1] https://www.bible.com/bible/1/REV.10.KJV Accessed January 8th, 2020 @08:12

The Seven Thunders

"The Seven Plagues"

The Seven thunders have been recorded by the ancients for thousands of years by the Hopis, the Yamassee and the Nuwaubians, have logged these thunders as a sign of the coming of a new planet, "Nibiru", the coming in of a new era, the sign of the end of the present world ruled by evil, and the resurrection of the ancient mysteries of Egypt, Atlantis rising again in the heart of Georgia, in a place called Wahanee. These signs are the signs of the times, recorded by the Ancient Neteru of Ancient Egypt, and passed down through time. They are called the thunders, or the plagues.

__First Thunders__: Much starvation, sickness, starving children, homelessness, and diseases. This already passed and continues.

__Second Thunders__: The sky becomes sick with holes in it, that look like sores, lung disease spreads, breathing problems occur, green mist comes from holes, polluting water, growing deformities, bacteria in the water (little devils), sea animals begin to die, fishes are trying to get out of the water, water becomes death to them. Physical and spiritual illness, mutations in animals.

__Third Thunder__: Many new species notations in animals, crossbreeding in species, death of frogs, honeybees, turtles, deformed human multiply, genetic splicing, and cloning.

__Fourth Thunder__: Sign of twins, Yah and Weh, one guards that south pole, and the other guards the north pole. Havoc

> begins with these poles, structures break down, Religion, Moral, and Financial. The Devil winds "El Nino" Takes over.
>
> **Fifth Thunder:** 4 Great People will perish. Floods, lightning, floods, tornados, landslides, hurricanes, hail in the summer, forest fires, children killing children, children killing their parents, rampant insanity and murders, and an upsurge in drug addiction, and demonic revivals parading themselves as righteous. El Nina, "Little Girl Will Come."
>
> **Sixth Thunder:** Changes Occur, The Star People return. Signs in the skies, New Planets, new galaxies, Meteorite Storms, Climatic Alterations, global warming, Spiritual Revivals, presence Of Divine, Disregard, and Respect for Present For World Governments, leadership, and politics.
>
> **Seventh Thunder:** The end of the world as you know it. The year 2030.[2]

These TIMES are UPON us NOW! I am sure that you are OBSERVANT to the ANOMALIES of this world?

There are many diseases, sicknesses, starvation, homelessness, and hunger in this world today, our skies are sick with holes and our waters are polluted, many new species of animals have popped up due to crossbreeding and experimentation, genetic splicing cloning, etc. There have been changes and anomalies at our north and south poles,

---

[2] http://holytablets.nuwaubianfacts.com/7thunders.htm Accessed January 8th, 2020 @08:17

there also appears to be a breakdown in the hierarchical structures which have been controlling this world for many years. People are waking up from their slumbers, many dropping their religions, and conforming to global consciousness. We are also experiencing adverse weather conditions and disasters including floods, hurricanes, and fires, etc.

Our children are killing each other every day. In our day we would fight and scrap and all would be well, but we would live to fight another day. It is not like this now as you are all aware. Instead of fistfights, children have turned to guns and knives. Where do all these knives and guns come from? There is also less loyalty on the street, many people are snitching on others to make a quick buck, cover their own backs, or even so they can receive a lesser custodial sentence. How things have changed? The star people are indeed returning. A spiritual awakening is occurring with people having an obvious disregard and respect for present world governments, leadership, and politics. Please watch out, you will be seeing and hearing about a lot of activities in space. It will come out in the movies first. **The world is changing as we know it!**

Please do YOUR RESEARCH and CHECK IT OUT FOR YOURSELF, don't just take it from me. Many people will not listen, they sit on the fence, bury their head in the sand, stick or adhere to the old systems and new technologies and monopolies which have been taking advantage of them, oppressing and even killing them.

There are going to be many CHANGES for the better but, of COURSE, THINGS WILL get WORSE before they get BETTER. This is NORMAL. YOU could CALL it a CHANGING of the GUARDS or even a CHANGING of the GODS, whatever interpretation you would like to use is fine but all I am saying is that BIG CHANGES are COMING. YOU WILL SEE if you are STILL AROUND, I am SURE. WATCH THIS SPACE!!!!! This is not something that I have just dreamt up, I assure YOU!

OUR LIVES are ALL about the LOVE and RESPECT that WE GIVE and the CHOICES that WE MAKE and the SERVICE in which WE give to OUR FAMILY, FRIENDS and other RELATIONS, which in turn dictates OUR JOURNEY on this PLANE. Please CORRECT me if I am WRONG. As WE KNOW, some changes will be good while others will be bad. This is completely NORMAL.

In this world, WE have GREATER MYSTERIES and LESSER mysteries. NOW IS THE TIME FOR ALL THESE MYSTERIES TO BE REVEALED. YOU WILL SEE!

The seven seals were broken in 1970 by a gentleman called Malachi Kobina Z. York, who brought to US the Holy Tablets. He renewed El's Holy Torah, El's Holy Injiyl, El's Holy Zabuwr, El's Holy Qur'an, the Holy Koran, circle seven, of the Moorish Holy Temple of Science, the problem book of the poor righteous teachers of this planet earth, The Egyptian Book of The Dead, Coming Forth by Day, and more. He has translated them from the original tongues so that WE ALL can be RENEWED.

Malachi does not get enough credit for what he has done for this PLAN-E.T. and HUMANITY. This is what has been happening to the BEST of US. The ONES that LIKE to DEAL with TRUTH ONLY. TRUTH is not ALWAYS PROFITABLE. SOME PEOPLE are only CONCERNED about PROFIT even if it is OVER LIVES. BUT THIS IS THE WAY of THE OLD WORLD, not the NEW ONE. CLING to the OLD WORLD and its HANDLERS, YOU WILL GET MESSED up, I assure YOU.

Did you SEE what happened to PRINCE ANDREW? What was he doing affiliating with MR EPSTEIN? And why did the

QUEEN sack him from royal duties? And what about Prince Harry and Meghan withdrawing from royal duties? There will be no Pope and no US president soon as those roles will no longer be required. Mark my WORDS!

NEW TIMES ARE HERE I TELL YOU – SOON YOU WILL KNOW.

Now is a TIME for PEACE, TRANSPARENCY, BALANCE, DIVINE LOVE, TRUTH, SERVICE, and ONENESS. WE MUST WORK IN THE ALL! (To learn more about this, I suggest you read Leon Moss's book, OMNIU. He breaks this down in great detail, how to work with the highest of oneself).

CHAPTER 2
MONOPOLIES

Source: [3]

"The days of MONOPOLIES will soon be OVER it will be a TIME of FREE TRADE FOR ALL."
— Kwadw(o) Naya, Baa Ankh Em Ra A'lyun Eil

---

3 Created by Charfilmax – https://www.pixabay.com

What is MONOPOLY?

Monopoly is a board game, a very famous board game in FACT. I am sure many of you have heard of it and are aware of the concept of the GAME. The goal of the board game MONOPOLY is to financially ruin your opponents through business and real estate purchases. The game is all about buying streets, building houses, and hotels then collect rent from the poor contestants landing on your properties and forcing them to foreclose if they cannot pay. Life can also be pretty much like this.

In business, the term monopoly refers to exclusive control of a commodity or service in a particular market, or a control that makes possible the manipulation of prices. [4]

> "**Monopoly** frequently... arises from government support or collusive agreements among individuals."
> — Milton Friedman

We do not need to worry, however, as the days of MONOPOLIES will soon be over, mark my words.

---

[4] https://www.dictionary.com/browse/monopoly Accessed December 6th, 2019 @07:01

"Kwadw(o), what makes you so sure about this?"

Don't worry I most often talk to myself; it keeps me happily insane or sane, whichever way you would like to look at it.

Let us take a look at the Fortune 500 companies.

What Is the Fortune 500?

The Fortune 500 is Fortune magazine's yearly list of 500 of the largest US companies ranked by total revenues for their respective fiscal years. The list is compiled using the most recent figures for revenue and includes both public and private companies with publicly available revenue data. To be a Fortune 500 company is widely considered to be a mark of prestige.

Although there used to be an ETF that tracked the Fortune 500 companies. there is currently no way to directly trade the stocks on the list as an index.

The Basics of the Fortune 500

The Fortune 500 survey includes companies that are incorporated and operate in the United States and file financial statements with government agencies—both publicly traded and privately held. It excludes private companies not filing financial statements with government agencies, foreign corporations, US companies consolidated by other companies, and companies that neglect to report full financial statements for at least three quarters of the current fiscal year.

As of 2019, companies are ranked by total revenues for their respective fiscal years as reported on their 10-K filings.

More than 1,800 American companies have been featured on the Fortune 500 list over the course of its history. The list has changed dramatically from the first Fortune 500 published in 1955. Mergers and acquisitions, shifts in production output, and bankruptcies have taken companies off of the list. The impact of a recession can also take out multiple companies from individual sectors. The Fortune 500 list can often be a telling sign of how strong the economy is or if there has been an economic recovery after poor performing years. [5]

Now let us take a quick look into the Fortune 500 list for the year 2018:

Fortune 500 2018

This year's Fortune 500 marks the 64th running of the list. In total, Fortune 500 companies represent two-thirds of the U.S. GDP with

---

[5] https://www.investopedia.com/terms/f/fortune500.asp Accessed December 6th, 2019 @07:20

$12.8 trillion in revenues, $1.0 trillion in profits, $21.6 trillion in market value, and employ 28.2 million people worldwide.[6]

Let us take a look at the top 10 companies on this list:

The Top 10

1. Walmart
2. Exxon Mobil
3. Berkshire Hathaway
4. Apple
5. UnitedHealth Group
6. McKesson
7. CVS Health
8. Amazon.com
9. AT&T
10. General Motors

Source: [7]

It is no surprise to see Walmart at number one or even to see Apple and Amazon at numbers 4 and 8, respectively. But

---

6 https://fortune.com/fortune500/2018/ Accessed December 6th, 2019 @07:30

7 https://fortune.com/fortune500/2018/ Accessed December 6th, 2019 @07:45

guess what? These companies will not last! I am not saying that they will go broke or bankrupt, but they most definitely will lose their monopolizations, mark my words. If you are lucky you will see it in your life before we reach the year 2031. You may think that I am talking CRAZY here, but I assure you my words are well substantiated.

Just take a look at the Fortune 500 list from 1900. Have you noticed something which backs up what I am saying here? Have you noticed that only sixteen of those companies are active today? No company is too BIG to FAIL! Look at Blackberry, for instance. There was a TIME when Blackberry phones were all the rage. You couldn't go into a business meeting without seeing loads of Blackberries on the tables, they were the 'IN' device for corporate workers and businesspeople. It seemed like most of the world was using the Blackberry Messenger Service, especially younger people who just had to exchange pins to keep in contact. How TIMES have CHANGED? I don't think anybody saw Blackberry failing.

Nokia was also dominant in the mobile phone market. You were not cool unless you had a NOKIA. Do you remember the NOKIA 3310? Where are they now? Then there was MySpace, the Facebook of that time. I am not sure if it still exists today, but it is funny how THINGS CHANGE so QUICK. Do you remember MySpace?

What about KODAK, do you remember those guys? They had a very big fall from grace. While making different cameras their chief product was film. KODAK had a MONOPOLY in their respective marketplace which was bigger than that of Coca Cola. But they made one very big mistake, which 'KILLED THEM' (which could happen to any company). They concentrated too much on one product concept that they missed out on dominating the technology in which THEY invented, digital photography. Where is KODAK now? What about Atari? What happened there? YOU SEE?

My prediction is that by 2031, monopolies will be a thing of the past. There will be no Queen or President running the country (it may well be out of business by then). There will also not be a Pope running Vatican City. But who am I to predict anything?

I would just like to leave you with the words of Ben Settle an extremely talented author and a world-class copywriter, you should read some of his books if you get the chance. He encapsulates why these big monopolies tend to fail – GREED. Please see the below emails that I have received from Ben on the 11ᵗʰ and 28ᵗʰ of November 2019. His views pretty much match up with my own in relation to this subject matter. I would be most interested to hear your thoughts to see if you see things in the same light:

> *"One of the many books I recommended to "Email Players" subscribers recently, is a book called "The Marvel Comics Story" by Sean Howe. Not so much as a "what to do" book. But, more of a "what NOT to do" book.*
>
> *As a long-time Marvel fan — decades before it became trendy to be a fan when all these recent fair-weather fans created by the Marvel movies were making fun of true comic book fans — I can tell you, the book is quite depressing in many ways. Overall, it was NOT the jovial place the late, great Stan Lee made it out to be in his monthly Stan's Soap Box column, with a happy and go-lucky bullpen of creators taking over the world.*
>
> *Yes, there was a lot of that in the '60s and '70s. But, come the '80s and beyond, it became a horror show of disappointment & despair, with broken lives, early deaths, and even outright suicides resulting in some cases. Why? The short answer is greed. As the company got bought by a string of ever-greedy publishers & stockholders who simply saw it as a cash cow to be picked clean of its meat at the expense of its soul, it turned into something that, today, is barely treading water compared to what it once was financially. The comic book side has become a huge joke full of inane wokeness and convoluted continuity, written by some of the most emotionally damaged & inept writers you'll ever see — with the movies & character*

licensing now being the main source of Marvel's income from what I can tell.

And if you think the movies are going to have a different fate, think again. It will likely still take some time. But, it's already going in the same direction under the watch of the Evil Mouse. And if you are paying attention to Star Wars' free-falling brand right now, that is but a taste of what awaits the Marvel brand.

The mindless fanboys will "LOL!!!!" at this because they are stupid. But, time always reveals all... which brings me to the point:

I once read a Chinese proverb from the great, and esteemed Matt Furey:

"A strength overextended becomes a weakness."

And if Marvel Comics ain't an example of that, I don't know what is.

One of the more fascinating phenomenon to see is how much short-term thinking fanboys of big tech, big media, big software, etc have, and how much they lack historical context.

For example:

I decided to start testing putting all my videos on Vimeo, instead of YouTube. A few curious souls asked out why I did this. And when I specifically told one of them one reason is I don't think YouTube is going to be what it is now forever... and I am weening myself away in advance... I got the typical amusing "I don't really have a point of view just feels" fanboy reply:

"LOL!!!!" Followed by a page or two of nonsensical text trying to justify their faith. The overachieving fanboy's rationalization hamster spinning was quite the spectacle, too. You could almost see the smoke from running so fast!

But here's the problem:

I hear tell YouTube alone lost some billion dollars last year. They are de-platforming some of their most influential users who bring in lots of traffic & de-monetizing people who think the wrong thoughts left and right. They are also under investigation for abusing children's data and keep flagrantly defying the feds — not to mention the many non-American governments gearing up to take a whack at 'em. And, if someone is short-sighted enough to think all that is a recipe for long term business success... or that YouTube is even in business to make a profit anymore vs imposing some kind of bat shyt social agenda then, well, be my guest, Maynard.

Same goes for Facebook fanboys and Twitter fanboys and Amazon fanboys. (Bezos himself declared they won't be around forever just a year ago.) And, especially Disney/Marvel fanboys — with all their inane wokeness they are going to be tripling down on going by the plans I've read about. In fact, Last Jedi — after making a mockery of the very things that made the Star Wars brand popular — did some $700 million less than expected. Yes, "it made a billion, Ben, LOL!!!" gross... but the net was an embarrassment for a major Star Wars movie. And if someone is foolish enough to believe the executives were sitting around celebrating & popping champagne for making almost a billion less than expected, for a sure-thing brand like Star Wars of all things... then that would be truly worthy of an LOL.

But those are just a couple examples.

When you look around you will see it everywhere:

Including giant "can't fail" brands sacrificing their brand power at the altar of the god of many virtue signals. Like Gillette (that lost close to $10 billion with a single #metoo-inspired advertisement)... ESPN (losing millions of viewers as they focus on scoring social justice points vs talking about, you know, sports)... Shea Moisture (there was a 100+ comment thread-hole in my old Facebook group a couple years ago, about their #EverybodyGetsLove campaign being a giant insult to the very demographic the company was founded to serve)... and the list goes on.

All these brands collectively took huge hits to their brands. Not necessarily fatal hits. But, a few more big ones and that could change... The point?

There is a whole host of other big brands that are, yes, right now as I type this, very big and seem invulnerable. But when you take even a cursory look at their numbers, their agendas, and the enormous piles of debt they rely on to keep going... not to mention number-fudging and accounting tricks by Shifty The Accountant in the back room... and how much they are butchering the very things that made their brands popular and flipping the bird to their core customers... you might just see how silly the "They are too big to fail LOL!!!!" secret gurus sound to anyone with a $5 calculator and a grasp of the last 100 years of business history."

I can relate to what Ben is saying here about big companies who have MONOPOLIES, which is the same thing that I was saying - the truth. **DIVINE TRUTH!** These large

CONGLOMERATES FAIL when they start TREATING their CUSTOMERS as nothing other than mere numbers and transactions who exist for no other reason than to make profits, opposed to the ETHICAL way of doing business which would be to find a way of serving and enhancing the lives of their customers.

Please let me KNOW your THOUGHTS.

CHAPTER 3
MIND CONTROL

Are you a MIND-CONTROLLED SLAVE?

Are you sure?

WHAT is MIND CONTROL?

Good question.

Let US TAKE a LOOK.

Source: [8]

Source: [9]

Most of us are in REALITY, MIND CONTROLLED SLAVES. Voluntarily for the most part. Our worlds,

---

8 From Pixabay
9 From Pixabay

KNOWLEDGE, LIFE, PERSPECTIVE, VIEWS, EVERYTHING has been given to US by EXTERNAL INSTRUCTION. TEL-LIE-VISION and Multi-Ethnic Destruction Information Agents are some of the MAIN PROPOGATERS of this MIND CONTROL.

Images and symbols play a huge part in our daily lives. YOU SEE WE INVEST in IMAGES and SYMBOLS. WE INVEST EMOTIONS and ENERGY; did YOU KNOW this?

At the very moment of writing this book (April 18th, 2020), the world is in CRISIS all except CHINA, who have just recovered. COVID-19 they call it. Now there is no better way to CONTROL a MASS POPULATION than by the UNITY of THOUGHT. For example, WE could CREATE an IMAGE of a FAKE PANDEMIC. Let's say WE called it COVID-19 and advertised it, symptoms and all through the internet, tv, radio, all mainstream media, creating PANIC, SHOCK, and FRENZY?

As YOU KNOW, WE have trained OUR SKILLED HEALTH PROFESSIONALS into OUR WAY of THINKING - they have ALL been to OUR SCHOOLS. WE don't have to worry, we trust them. They will SELL OUR MESSAGE to the SHEEPLE and the SHEEPLE trust them.

WE globalists couldn't care less about THE virus. We're only using the IDEA, the IMAGE of it, to scare the population, spreading, FEAR, STRESS, PANIC, and ANXIETY amongst the masses. Leaving the SHEEPLE with no TIME to CRITICALLY THINK or ANALYZE. Most are too busy SLEEPING in any case. YOU SEE, when they are like this, they are EASIER to CONTROL, WE NEED to keep them BLINDED, RUSHED, PANICKED or SHOCKED, it is always best.

WE will get the people scared with the IMAGE that WE have CREATED, a COVID-19 PANDEMIC. Backing away. Shutting their doors. OUR MEDIA boys will take care of it nicely. They will TRANSMIT the appropriate IMAGES at the appropriate FREQUENCIES down their different CHANNELS to PROGRAM the SHEEPLE (TEL.LIE.VISION is particularly good for this). They will be pounded by drug commercials around the clock. These ads will claim that hundreds and hundreds of symptoms of COVID-19 are loose in the world and require immediate diagnosis and treatment by way of VACCINATION. If the PANDEMIC or EPIDEMIC gets OUT of CONTROL, we can always INTRODUCE MANDATORY VACCINATIONS for EVERYONE except US, WHAT DO YOU THINK?

All in the name of SCIENCE.

FAKE SCIENCE.

PANDEMIC, PANDEMIC, READ ALL ABOUT IT!!!!!!

It is the best way to keep money, have fun, and stay in control, are you with me on this one? For US to KNOW and for them to FIND OUT (I wonder how long it will take them?). Soon they will all be running out to get the VACCINE because of the IMAGE that WE have CREATED, a fake IMAGE, which is based around FAKE SCIENCE. Isn't that MIND CONTROL in its highest FORM? YOU SEE WE CANNOT LOSE!

WE profit from the sale of drugs and vaccines. WE also PROFIT from the ON-GOING PERSCRIPTIONS, they will take what WE PRESCRIBE to them and GROW to LOVE it, WANT it, NEED it. They make it so ADDICTIVE that they have us running back for more. I THINK that WE are missing something here. Maybe missing a trick or something here?

Maybe we should encourage mass lockdowns and alienate people from each other. Maybe they will trust each other less as a result of less social interaction or is it more a case of social exclusion? Television

The lockdowns plus the television would CREATE the PERFECT IMAGE of a PANDEMIC. It would FOCUS people on the NEED to be VACCINATED and give them a REASON for them to come under OUR CONTROL. Don't WORRY, WE have ALLIANCES with ALL MAJOR PHARMACEUTICAL companies and ALL WORLD GOVERNMENTS, BELONG to US in some shape or form. We control the money, the resources, the food, drugs, medicine, and the sheeple – just the way we like it. There is nothing worse than having dissidents in the ranks is there, now?

WE HAVE UNIFIED THE MINDS of the PEOPLE and have CREATED THEIR THOUGHTS through the MEDIUM of SYMBOLS and FAKE IMAGERY, INSTILLING, FEAR, and SUFFERING. This is normal, WE are the ARCHITECTS. WE have the POWER as LONG as the SHEEPLE are going to INVEST their EMOTIONS into IMAGES without CLARIFYING the FACTS FIRST or even at ALL. They are never going to TAKE what is OURS, what WE have FOUGHT so LONG and HARD for, are you crazy?

Long live the Cabal!!!!

Long live the Cabal!!!!

WE CREATE PANDEMIC upon discovering a NEW HIGHLY CONTAGIOUS and INFECTIOUS VIRUS. Our diagnostic tests which are worthless but open the door to the phony escalation of case numbers. On top of that, we collate many people who have DIFFERENT traditional diseases but display the same or similar symptoms under the meaningless umbrella term, "COVID-19"; the plan to introduce our profitable toxic vaccine as the "solution." Sounds good if you ask me, what would you say?

Long live the Cabal!!!!

Long live the Cabal!!!!

IMAGES and SYMBOLS are VERY IMPORTANT as HUMANS INVEST EMOTIONS into THEM often without KNOWING, without REALIZATION. Can YOU SEE where I am coming from? There are a lot more examples of this which I will go through another time.

CHAPTER 4
FROM A.I. TO A.G.I.

Source: [10]

"We humans are not just pattern recognizers. We're also building models about the things we see."
– Dileep George (Co-founder of Vicarious)

---

[10] Created by Geralt – https://www.pixabay.com

AI (Artificial Intelligence) is very popular today; WE SEE it EVERYWHERE. AI companies appear to be popping up ALL OVER the place. I mentioned in the last book (Choices) that the robots keep taking OUR jobs, this is most true. Maybe it is necessary? Maybe we humans are no good for work? Maybe WE are too lazy? Or WE make too many mistakes? Maybe WE are just USELESS? Who KNOWS? I don't run or control the world.

Many people believe that Bill Gates promotes vaccinations as a way of controlling and reducing the population because of the problems that WE are facing in the world. He believes that there are too many people using up too many resources and that this is not sustainable for much longer. Many of his trillionaire and billionaire buddies share the same sentiment.

Jeff Bezos thinks along similar lines, but he FEELS that maybe WE can find more resources on other planets within our solar system. He is currently investing in the Blue Origin project and is also currently involved with Project Kuiper, a Satellite broadband venture which involves putting more than 3,200 satellites in low Earth orbit for global broadband coverage. Check all these things out for yourself!

What is AI?

Good question.

In layman's terms, AI is any task performed by a program or a machine that if a human carried out the same activity, we would say the human had to apply intelligence to accomplish the task. This definition is very broad in perspective, I know, so is LIFE, hence all the anomalies and grievances. AI robots and systems tend to demonstrate or mimic human behaviors associated with human intelligence such as planning, learning, reasoning, problem-solving, knowledge representation, perception, motion but they struggle with CREATIVITY.

At present, there are two types of AI: narrow AI and AGI. Narrow AI is commonplace today, we see it everywhere. We have intelligent systems that have learned to carry out specific tasks without being explicitly programmed. From speech and language recognition systems such as Siri, Amazon Echo and Alexa, and the Google speech to text app, to such things like interpreting video feeds from drones, carrying out visual inspections of infrastructure, responding to simple customer-service queries, coordinating with other intelligent systems to carry out tasks like booking a hotel at a suitable time and location, helping radiologists to spot potential tumors in Xrays, flagging inappropriate content online, detecting wear and tear in elevators from data gathered by IoT devices, the list goes on and on. There are many existing and emerging applications for AI in this new age which is upon US.

But what about AGI?

That is also a good question.

What is AGI? Is it possible? Is there a need for it? These are all very good questions. It is good to be in a position to WITNESS and OBSERVE how TIMES are CHANGING. But are these CHANGES for the BETTER or the WORSE? Who KNOWS? Do YOU? Do YOU CARE? What impact are the CHANGES going to HAVE on US ALL? On US and OUR CHILDREN and OUR CHILDREN'S CHILDREN? What is going to happen next?

With **AGI** (Artificial General Intelligence) we enter a whole new ball game. AGI relates to the adaptable intellect found in humans, which would give machines and robots a flexible form of intelligence capability, which would then enable them to learn and adapt just like us humans do.

AGI is commonly seen in movies such as:

- The Terminator
- Ex Machina
- A.I. Artificial Intelligence
- 2001: A Space Odyssey
- Metropolis
- I, Robot
- The Matrix Series
- RoboCop
- Short Circuit
- Austin Powers: International Man Of Mystery
- Blade Runner
- The Machine
- Star Wars
- Star Trek: Generations

But it does not exist in the world today at present well, not to my knowledge. If you have any updates on this, please let me know. I would be most interested to hear.

Many experts say that AGI will be developed and implemented in the near future. Yet, other experts say that AGI is not possible. Isn't anything possible? You see the human body is a very sophisticated bit of equipment, to this date I have not seen a bit of equipment which matches up to it. Gratification must go to the CREATOR. GOOD JOB. WE

MUST GIVE CREDIT WHERE IT IS DUE AND FOR THIS I WOULD LIKE TO GIVE THANKS TO THE MOST HIGH (EL KULUWM), PLEASE FEEL FREE TO JOIN ME.

Technology is great but to this day I have not seen any technology that has FREE WILL like us HUMANS. I haven't seen technology that has FEELINGS or EMOTIONS or even any that have any advanced adaptive learning capabilities. AGI robots may be great for learning patterns and trends, for working out algorithms, or for automation and multitasking. However, at this point, we cannot remove human beings from the equation as the machines and robots are simply not up to the job at the moment.

What are your thoughts on this matter? Are we going to reproduce amongst ourselves to CREATE MORE LIFE? Or are WE going to SEE a NEW ERA in which CYBORG people will replace US as the dominant species on this earth? Are WE the dominant species of the EARTH? According to US, WE are but MAYBE the ALIENS THINK different. Who knows? I guess you need to ask them. But to THINK that WE are the MOST DOMINANT and INTELLIGENT SPECIES on this PLAN-E.T. is going too far. But who am I to say anything of this nature?

Have you heard of Neuralink? Neuralink is one of Elon Musk's new ventures, his brain-computer interface company. They are inventing mind-controlled gadgets for the masses. Neuralink have been involved with great AGI research, exploring the properties and links between neuroscience and AI. This project in question, if successful, would SEE people using thought-controlled robots in their everyday lives Such as a thought-controlled robotic arm. Can you imagine how they have been testing this concept? I have heard that they should be ready for human trials by 2020, which is some time this year. How times are changing! Nothing has gone mainstream yet, but investments and developments are being made in this area more-so every day.

I just would like to finish off this chapter by making a few observations. I would like to start by asking you a few questions. Where are WE going to go in this LIFE? Which CHOICE or CHOICES are WE going to MAKE? What are our preferences? Is it TRUE that the ERA of HUMAN INFLUENCE over this PLAN-E.T. is about to come to an end as prophesized? Is the AGE of super-intelligent beings about to begin? What would happen if this were the case? I can see many potential ISSUES.

In Estonia, they have been experimenting with AI judges which should be in place sometime this year. These AI judges would be stationed in small claims courts in Estonia to moderate disputes of less than 7000 Euros. I feel sorry for the ladies and gentlemen who end up in court. I would never want my fate to be decided by a machine or computer. Even in the US, algorithms are being used in sentencing decisions. If you don't believe me, check it out for yourself.

I am not a technologist, machinist, or roboticist. I don't believe in mechanism and robotics. It is each to their own but I tend to stick to nature, don't you?

Before I finish off this chapter, I would like to leave you with the comments of Aled Jenkins (BabbleBrick CEO) and Dane Walters, a data scientist, who speaks about the future possibilities of AI.

> *Aled Jenkins (September 20th, 2019)*
>
> "AI Future Possibilities:
>
> 1. We can control AI through their code and they become our most powerful tool.

2. AI is used as the ultimate weapon in war. This would lead to unimaginable terror.

3. We live peacefully alongside AI as equals.

4. AI develop their own goals, which we are not a part of. They end up killing or controlling us.

5. We integrate with them i.e. we have AI implanted into our bodies.

6. AGI is impossible."

Dane Walters (September 21st, 2019)

"As a data scientist who makes AIs for work... I can't help but sigh at the sensationalism here. In its current state, indeed with the current way we're working on it, AI can't do what you want it to.

All any modern AI is statistically fitting. Very, very complicated statistical fitting, but that's what it is nonetheless. What you're describing will require multiple compute and other paradigm shifts and revolutions that would be akin to a US supercarrier getting hand-delivered to a caveman.

Our strongest supercomputers can't even simulate 1% of your brain's neurons and connections; nowhere near it in fact. We're increasingly discovering that the way our "neural networks" function isn't even how your brain does things, it's based on outdated science from the 50s and 60s, which, by the way, is when the modern neural network concept was originally fleshed out.

In order to get an AGI, our computers will need to be thousands of times faster and more complex than they are. They will require as of now yet undeveloped physical structures to enable that fast computation. It's a pipe dream for now.

No, actually, it's below that. It's a caveman trying to build an aircraft carrier. We simply don't know enough, don't even think correctly, and don't have the resources to even get close.

*We can't solve the problem of universal object detection. Take any image net classifier and hand it a picture you've taken. Just a random one. It will absolutely **fail**. Take a picture it succeeds on and add 3% Gaussian noise to it; largely imperceptible to you. It will **fail**. Our current AI and our current computers are sticks and stones when we need nuclear reactors and rolled steel.*

I really really really wish they'd called neural networks and AI something, anything, else, so this kind of nonsense didn't get proliferated."

I am sure that you are aware of the topic we speak, if not, hopefully, you have taken something from it. I just wanted to highlight this new anomaly so we can look at things from a mixture of perspectives. WE ALL must have an OVERSTANDING of the WORLD(S) around us, which would give us the CORRECT INTERPRETATIONS of LIFE. It is only then that WE would have the capability to make CORRECT JUDGEMENTS.

THIS LIFE IS ABOUT CHOICES. WHICH CHOICE IS FOR YOU? NATURAL NATURE or TRANSHUMANISM?

CHAPTER 5
COGNITIVE DISSONANCE

"A man who views the world the same at fifty as he did at twenty has wasted thirty years of his life."
— *Muhammad Ali*

Cognitive dissonance isn't something we talk about a lot, but we experience it all the time. It is a BIG PROBLEM in the WORLD TODAY. When one KNOWS they KNOW, but sadly most people suffer from this condition UNKNOWINGLY, SUBCONSCIOUSLY as if they are MENTALLY DEAD.

What is this cognitive dissonance that WE SPEAK off?

Cognitive dissonance is a conditional behavior trait that was first noticed by Leon Festinger (an American social psychologist) around 1957. Leon Festinger's observation of a cult that believed that the earth was going to be destroyed by a flood led to the introduction of the concept. In the study, when the flood didn't come, a lot of the fringe members of the realized that they had 'been taken for a ride' and realized that they had been fooled. However, the hardcore members of the cult did not see it this way.

Many of the cult members had given up their homes, jobs, and lives to work for the cult. These cult members re-interpreted the evidence in their own way, putting things down to FAITH. They believed that the lack of a flood was due to the actions and UNFAITHFULNESS of the cult members. Imagine that? It is like a smoker who KNOWS that smoking KILLS but then they find a nice WAY of JUSTIFYING it. They

KNOW that smoking causes cancer, heart attacks, and lung disease, which is COGNITION, however, they are in a STATE of COGNITIVE DISSONANCE. Another example is a parent who takes their child to the doctors for vaccinations, even though they know that vaccinations are very harmful to children. I can THINK of so many examples of this, I am sure that you can too.

Examples of situations where cognitive dissonance can occur include such things as:

- Choosing to promote a behavior, such as regular exercise, that a person does not themselves practice. This type of cognitive dissonance is called *hypocrisy*.
- Telling a lie despite the person thinking of themselves as honest.
- Purchasing a new car that is not fuel-efficient, despite being environmentally conscious.
- Eating meat while also thinking of themselves as an animal lover who dislikes the thought of killing animals.[11]

---

11 https://www.medicalnewstoday.com/articles/326738.php#examples Accessed January 29th, 2020.

When people display action or traits of cognitive dissonance it tends to make them **FEEL**, angry, guilty, ashamed, which as a result, causes the person in question to try and hide their actions or beliefs from others or they try to justify their actions especially at times where their actions and choices are unjustifiable. Sometimes they will shy away from conversations or debates about specific topics or avoid learning any new information, ignoring research, facts, divine truth, doctors' advice, basically anything that would cause them dissonance or go against their core beliefs.

Most of US suffer from cognitive dissonance, this SICKNESS often causes US to CHANGE OUR **behaviors** and **actions** to align with OUR BELIEFS. Ignoring the facts and holding onto religion is a PRIME example of this. Most people will fight to defend their religion(s) if FACTS and TRUTHS are SET against the CORE BELIEFS of the teachings and doctrine in question.

Cognitive dissonance is the MENTAL conflict that occurs when OUR beliefs and assumptions are contradicted by new information. It is difficult for US to consciously and unconsciously drop our old ways and accept that THEY are wrong. Often, WE tend to preserve OUR current understanding, defending rejecting, explaining away, or avoiding any new information that comes against it. Sometimes people experiencing cognitive dissonance even convince themselves that no conflict exists.

According to Leon Festinger (1957), cognitive dissonance is the feeling of discomfort produced by the presence of two thoughts that are in conflict with one another.

It is TRUE!

It is commonplace to SEE people holding CORE BELIEFS that are very strong. It is also commonplace to SEE these very same people LOOKING or ACTING very uncomfortable when they are presented with new evidence that works against these BELIEFS. They FEEL a NEED within themselves to PROTECT that CORE BELIEF. THIS IS A PROBLEM WHICH AFFECTS THE MENTALLY DEAD WITHIN OUR SOCIETIES, but the CURE is QUITE SIMPLE.

BELIEF is not the answer, WE SHOULD KNOW! If WE don't KNOW, WHY should WE TALK and give an opinion on things as if we are an EXPERT. If WE don't KNOW something WE should FIND OUT. KNOWLEDGE is POWER. WISDOM is BLISS. IGNORANCE is BLIND, it can also be very PAINFUL.

So many people are armed with FAKE KNOWLEDGE from the TEL-LIE-VISION and the media. It is very SAD. Do people not READ BOOKS anymore?

I would like to finish this chapter by leaving you with a few quotes. I am not religious in any way shape or form, but I find these quotes quite fitting.

> *"Beliefs have the power to create and the power to destroy. Human beings have the awesome ability to take any experience of their lives and create a meaning that disempowers them or one that can literally save their lives."*
> — Tony Robbins

> *"My people are destroyed for lack of knowledge: because thou hast rejected knowledge, I will also reject thee, that thou shalt be no priest to me: seeing thou hast forgotten the law of thy God, I will also forget thy children."*
> — *Hosea 4:6 (New King James Version)*

> *"Where there is no vision, the people perish: but he that keepeth the law, happy is he."*
> — *Proverbs 29:18 Hosea 4:6 (King James Version)*

CHAPTER 6
L.G.B.T.Q. AGENDAS

Source: [12]

"If I Came Back to the U.S., I Would Likely Die in Prison for Telling the Truth."[13]
— *Edward Snowden*

---

12 Created by Cecilie Johnsen – https://www.unslash.com
13 https://www.democracynow.org/2019/12/5/edward_snowden_amy_goodman_interview_sweden Accessed December 9th, 2019 @17:54

I saw the following posts on Chief Nanya Shaabu Eil's Facebook account last year. Please SEE the screenshot below and let me know what YOU THINK.

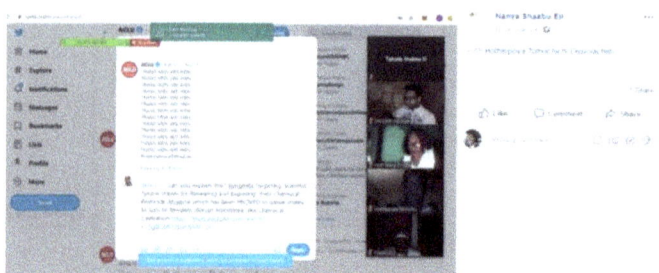

You can see that Nanya Shaabu Eil was blocked on Twitter. He was suspended when he started defending scientist, Tyrone Hayes.

Please check out the Chiefs' comment below:

"@ACLU - can you explain this? Syngenta Targeting Scientist Tyrone Hayes for Revealing and Exposing their Chemical Pesticide Atrazine which has been PROVED to cause males to turn to females; disrupt hormones, aka Chemical Castration." https://www.youtube.comwatch?v=SgBCMO3EuHM&t=3s

For the record, the YouTube video appears to have been taken down also, funny if you ask me.

I don't THINK that the CHIEF was saying anything DEROGATORY, do YOU? I FEEL that his LINE of QUESTIONING CORRECT, what would you say?

Who is Tyrone Hayes? Have you ever heard of him? I suggest YOU GOOGLE him, but first, check out this short extract:

> *Silencing the Scientist: Tyrone Hayes on Being Targeted by Herbicide Firm Syngenta Story - February 21st, 2014*
>
> "We speak with scientist Tyrone Hayes of the University of California, Berkeley, who discovered a widely used herbicide may have harmful effects on the endocrine system. But when he tried to publish the results, the chemical's manufacturer launched a campaign to discredit his work. Hayes was first hired in 1997 by a company, which later became agribusiness giant Syngenta, to study their product, atrazine, a pesticide that is applied to more than half the corn crops in the United States, and widely used on golf courses and Christmas tree farms. When Hayes found results Syngenta did not expect — that atrazine causes sexual abnormalities in frogs, and could cause the same problems for humans — it refused to allow him to publish his findings. A new article in The New Yorker magazine uses court documents from a class-action lawsuit against Syngenta to show how it sought to smear Hayes' reputation and prevent the U.S. Environmental Protection Agency from banning the profitable chemical, which is already banned by the European Union.

Please check out the rest of the conversation that got the Chief banned from TWITTER for LIFE. I do not SEE anything WRONG in his DIALOGUE here, DO YOU?

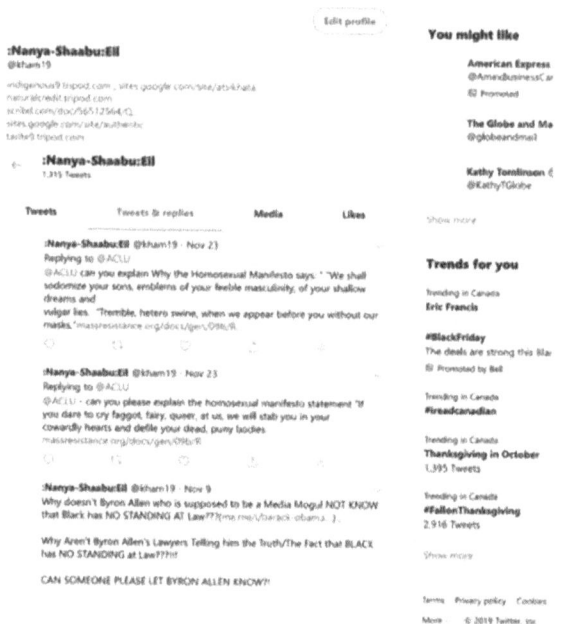

Choices 2

11/28/2019   Gmail - Case# 0133481142: Appealing an account suspension - @kham19 [ref:_00DA0K0A8._5004A1pMl13:ref]

 Gmail   :Nanya :Eli <kemit19@gmail.com>

Case# 0133481142: Appealing an account suspension - @kham19 [ref:_00DA0K0A8._5004A1pMl13:ref]

support@twitter.com <support@twitter.com>   Thu, Nov 28, 2019 at 1:00 AM
To: "kemit19@gmail.com" <kemit19@gmail.com>

Hello,

After investigating your appeal, we have determined that your account posted content that was threatening and/or promoting violence in violation of the Twitter Terms of Service. Accordingly, your account has been suspended and will not be restored.

You can learn more about suspended accounts here: https://help.twitter.com/managing-your-account/suspended-twitter-accounts.

Thanks,

Twitter

Help | Privacy

Twitter, Inc. 1355 Market Street, Suite 900 San Francisco, CA 94103

ref:_00DA0K0A8._5004A1pMl13:ref

https://mail.google.com/mail/u/2?ik=f7e54871ad&view=pt&search=all&permmsgid=msg-f%3A165143172535050808408simpl=msg-f%3A16514317253... 1/1

Please read the Chief's comments:

> "Abdur Kull Shaayuaat Bi Wah Saamus Pa Temt-Ta
>
> Begin All Things By First Using The All
>
> It's OFFICIAL! Twitter.com is under control of the Homosexual Manifesto!
>
> On November 23, 2019. I posed a question to ACLU regarding the Homosexual Manifesto By Michael Swift, "Gay Revolutionary." Reprinted from The Congressional Record of the United States Congress. First printed in Gay Community News, February 15-21 1987 which is on https://www.massresistance.org/.../Re.../chapters/Chapter-13.pdf.
>
> I asked the ACLU (since they said Transmen are Men on International Men's Day) to explain why in the Homosexual Manifesto that they would: "We shall sodomize your sons, emblems of your feeble masculinity, of your shallow dreams and vulgar lies."
>
> Further: "If you dare to cry faggot, fairy, queer, at us, we will stab you in your cowardly hearts and defile your dead, puny bodies." and Further: "Tremble, hetero swine, when we appear before you without our masks."
>
> These are statements made by Homosexual Activists and published in the US Congress in 1987. The Statements would be considered uttering threats, genocide, apartheid and crimes against humanity.

I merely quote what was said by Homosexual/Gay Activists which is published by the US Government.

Why is My [twitter] account being suspended for the ACLU clearly being unable to answer my question? This does not violate twitter community standards.

This PROVES the Homosexual Manifesto/Agenda is REAL! and ANYONE who Questions it threatens the Protocols (Plans) of the Learnt Elders of Zion."[14]

Have you ever heard of N.A.M.B.L.A.?

Please check out the following two extracts:

*"**North American Man/Boy Love Association - Wikipedia***

https://en.wikipedia.org/wiki/North_American_Man/Boy_Love_Association

*The North American Man/Boy Love Association (**NAMBLA**) is a paedophilia and pederasty advocacy organization in the United States. It works to abolish age-of-consent laws criminalizing adult sexual involvement with minors and campaigns for the release of men who have been jailed for*

---

14 https://www.facebook.com/Nanya.Shaabu.EiL/posts/10212833864321508?__xts__[0]=68.ARA4v2z7uDLopQ163mlıPw4FaJVq6mKEt5tHc9I-fYmMqTVMaONFGu-htT4J1XEJLw9Xvh6M6TzPk6NXJ9AbFYcuod6p ZM6HtidbRkIfQUB4NMzl4qKSDyjAXm_AnnSXkoItBv-3-PJptTjo-CP9-TJfo246nKFkN2dyGirn_5EZ1OQTesOtJtDNGHWJRq7P_ve37iccn9TiSEINu A&__tn__=-R Accessed December 9th, 2019 @13:19

sexual contacts with minors that did not involve what it considers coercion."

"Urban Dictionary: NAMBLA

htttps://www.urbandictionary.com/define-php?term=NAMBLA

The National Man-Boy Love Association. They are a group of men, mostly over 30, who like to date/have sex with underage boys. They like to use historical "evidence" like how in ancient Greece, this sort of thing was tolerated, to try and support their movement. (They also like to take text from books, out of context, to support their movement, the author unaware of their doing so, thus making ..."[15]

And what is going on with this?

---

[15] https://duckduckgo.com/?t=palemoon&q=nambla&ia=web Accessed April 19th, 2020 @19:41

Choices 2

Source: 16

"New Jersey law to require schools to teach LGBT history in class.

TRENTON, New Jersey - New Jersey has become the second state in the nation after California to pass a law requiring schools to teach LGBT history in their classrooms.

Under the new measure, public schools must include lessons about the political, economic, and social contributions of the LGBT community.

The new law goes into effect at the beginning of the 2020 school year.Gov. Phil Murphy called the law a step towards inclusion and fairness.This legislation comes as the #ExposeChristianSchools hashtag started trending on Twitter. It was introduced shortly after news broke that Karen Pence,

---

16 https://www.facebook.com/Wepwawet9/posts/10158331277145200 Accessed April 19th, 2020 @19:47

> wife of Vice President Mike Pence, would be teaching at a Christian school in northern Virginia that lists "homosexual or lesbian sexual activity" as among the disqualifying criteria for prospective employees."[17]

Well, it LOOKS like WE have a new movement in TOWN. The L.G.B.T.Q.E.P.B.Z. Movement. I call them the ALPHABET PEOPLE. When I was young things were a little different. Gay meant happy and most people were heterosexual or straight as you would call it back then. There were a few people who were confused about their gender and sexuality.

Now it is a whole different ball game, the ALPHABET PEOPLE even have their own flag. The flag is made up of the colors of OUR CHAKRAS. How Strange. I do not mind what people are, that is up to them. If a man wants to have a loving relationship with his animal, then that is up to him. As long as he knows that it will be impossible for him to bring life into the world. WE are all entitled to our preferences. But we cannot cheat nature. To keep our species ALIVE, WE NEED to REPRODUCE. OUR WORLDS would END if there were no new babies been born.

---

[17] https://abc13.com/education/law-to-require-schools-to-teach-lgbt-history-in-class/5120283/?sf207209673=1&fbclid=IwAR3SQOl6q2fBCihxZCc9iUbxLdhY_ldyN5ICfAz4a_jrA0yiUYaOJSusbKw Accessed April 19th, 2020 @19:56

This L.G.B.T.Q.E.P.B.Z. Movement, what is it about? Let us take a look SEE:

> "LGBTQA+
>
> Initialism that stands for Lesbian, Gay, Bisexual, Transgender, Queer, Asexual, the + alludes to other sexual orientations like Pansexual."[18]
>
> "The Cult of LGBTQE-E for EVIL and is often a cover for child-molesting perverts.
>
> Tagged Under: abuse, children's health, gender-confused, gender issues, gender madness, the left cult, LGBTQE, un-godly Mob, Lunacy, mutilation, transgender, Child molesting perverts LGBTQE- E For Evil, drag queens, perverts
>
> Unfortunately, not all alternative sources are reliable, even some Major Christian (and I use Christian loosely) news sources have been corrupted. They will NOT tell the truth. They just parrot the deceptive narratives perpetrated by those who currently control our government and media. Even those who are honestly trying to present the truth can miss it sometimes. There is so much deception out there. In these last days, you must be wise as serpents and gentle as lambs. It is no time to sleep or slumber. Diligence and vigilance are required. It is critical that you think for yourself and not be a Lemming."[19]

---

18 https://www.urbandictionary.com/define.php?term=LGBTQA%2B Accessed April 19th, 2020 @20:33

19 https://hnewswire.com/un-lgbtqe-e-is-for-evil-czar-takes-aim-against-religions/ Accessed April 19th, 2020 @20:35

When I was young, life was ever so simple, we all had much fewer CHOICES to make. LIFE seems ever so COMPLEX these days. What do YOU THINK? Take a look at the list below.

List of Genders

- Men
- Women
- All genders
- Agender
- Androgynes
- Bigender
- Cis Men
- Cis Women
- Genderfluid
- Genderqueer
- Genders Nonconforming
- Hijras
- Intersexes
- Non-binary
- Others
- Pangender
- Transfeminine
- Transgender
- Transmasculine
- Transsexuals
- Transmen
- Transwomen
- Two Spirits

This is a list of genders that we have today, please let me know if I have missed any out. For me, it is all a bit too confusing. I would be interested to know YOUR THOUGHTS. It is each to their own, I say. Everyone is entitled to their fun and their preferences. But it is best that everyone KNOWS what they are doing. For example, some people get sex changes, especially at a very early age, and regret it later. This happens many times. I am sure that you have heard a few cases if this? To prevent this, people need to KNOW what they are doing so that they have no REGRETS.

WE should also consider the FUTURE.

NO BABIES MEANS NO FUTURE!

CHAPTER 7A
UFOs, IFOs, AND OOTWFOs

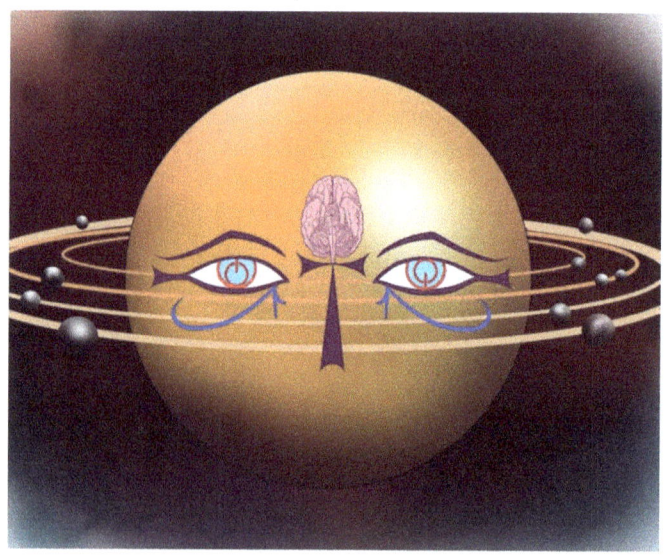

"You can fool some of the people sometimes, but you can't fool all the people all of the time"
— *Malachi Z. York*

UFOs, IFOs, and OOTWFOs – what is the first thing that springs to your MIND? The first thing that sprung to mind is WHAT ARE THESE THINGS? I am sure WE ALL KNOW what a UFO is but WHAT is an IFO and an OOTWFO?

Do you MIND if I ask YOU a few QUESTIONS? Do YOU THINK that WE are alone in this WORLD? How likely is it that other civilizations are living here on this PLAN-E.T. without our knowledge? Do ALIENS exist? What is an ALIEN? Are ALIENS EXTRA-TERRESTRIAL, is there a DIFFERENCE? Very good questions, if you ask me!

Let US start with UFOs. UFOs are known as Unidentified Flying Objects. Now people tend to confuse UFOs with aliens. When they see or hear about a UFO, they often conflate the concept with the idea of whether or not we have been visited by aliens. A UFO is what it is - an unidentified flying object. But it is **NOT** actually OUT OF THIS WORLD! As you can SEE, the term UFO is very non-specific which kind of admits that we do not know what we are looking at. THINK about it. Could this be so, for a reason?

We all know that the universe brings mysteries and just because WE do not know what WE are looking at does not necessarily mean that aliens have been visiting us. If one does not KNOW what they are LOOKING at, it is obvious that they can never say it is anything as they do not KNOW. This is really simple stuff. A UFO in simple man's terms is simply just a flying object in which WE know nothing about. One that has been unidentified but is still from within this world. THINK about it, if something is unidentified, it usually implies nothing about its makeup, origins, or validity. It just means 'don't know' and there always seem to be many things that we don't KNOW. What do YOU FEEL? Are YOU with me on this one?

I was reading a book recently by Nick Pope who worked for the Ministry of Defense investigating UFO sightings between 1991 and 1994. The book is titled:

"Are They Really Here? The Uninvited. An Expose Of The Alien Abduction Phenomenon."

I must admit it was quite a good, interesting read. I have read through it a few times now. It relates mainly to abductions and visitations of an extra-terrestrial nature, and it also touches on UFOs and justifying their relation to OOTWFOs. It is well worth reading.

Let us check out a little extract:

"All around the world, quite independently, thousands of people claim that they have been abducted by aliens. At first sight, these claims seem ludicrous, but when one takes a closer look, it soon becomes clear that they are supported by some very convincing evidence. Clearly, something strange is going on. But what, exactly? I spent three years of my life in a job where my duties included investigating UFO sightings for the Ministry of Defence. Between 1991 and 1994 my duties at the Ministry involved me in a search for the truth about one of the most powerful and enduring mysteries of modem times.

My first book, Open Skies, Closed Minds, told the story of my three-year voyage of discovery, and detailed some of what television devotees might like to think of as "the real X-Files." I had come into the job as a skeptic but emerged believing that a small percentage of UFO sightings did involve extra-terrestrial craft. My conversion was not a blind leap of faith but was based upon numerous instances where my rigorous official investigations had failed to uncover any conventional explanation for what was seen. These cases included visual sightings backed up by radar evidence, and UFO reports from civil and military pilots.

In 1980 there was a case where radiation readings ten times normal were recorded on the spot where a metallic craft landed near two military bases (the famous Rendlesham Forest case). In 1990 the Belgian Air Force scrambled F-16 fighters to try and intercept a UFO that had been picked up on radar by various NATO and Belgian installations, but the UFO easily evaded the jets. In 1993 a craft flew directly over two Royal Air Force bases in England, firing a beam of light at the surrounding countryside. There were plenty of cases where the intruding technology seemed to be considerably more advanced than the *defending technology. Fascinating and disturbing though some of these UFO incidents were, it was always the reports of abductions that gave me the greatest concern. The UFO mystery paled into insignificance when compared to the abduction phenomenon. Although there will be much talk about extra-terrestrials, I should make it clear that this book is not about UFOs. Although, of course, UFOs will be featured, the central issue here is encounters between humans and other, non-human intelligences. Using an analogy to illustrate the point, if the Queen called at your house, you would probably not be that interested in the car in which she arrived. You would want to know why she was visiting you! In the same way, for those like me who believe that some UFOs are extra-terrestrial in origin, the UFOs become, simply, a means of transportation. As the respected ufologist Stanton Friedman has said: "Never mind the saucers; what about the occupants?" For me, carrying out my job at the Ministry, the whole issue of alien abductions raised serious defense and national security issues. If the accounts were to be believed, then not only were UFOs penetrating our sophisticated air defense network with impunity, but the occupants of the craft were sometimes carrying out intrusive and frightening procedures on unwilling human subjects. When I first encountered references to alien abductions, I was skeptical. Similarly, when I was actually introduced to people who claimed that they had been abducted, I found myself looking for other, more conventional explanations. Were they simply lying, or were they fantasy-prone personalities, who might construct an abduction story for psychological reasons? Might there be mental health explanations, with some sort of psychopathology lying at the root of these people's claims? Could it be that certain stimuli had combined to create mass hysteria on a frightening scale? All these options needed to be explored, and would in*

> themselves have been worthy of serious study. But the most frightening theory of all was that the claims were true, and the events were occurring as described.
>
> If they were true-if just one case was true - the implications for the human race would be profound and disturbing. It is clear that, despite the unwelcome intrusion of various cranks, most of the so-called abductees who have come forward to talk about their experiences are sincere and well-intentioned. For this reason, although I believe that many such experiences do have conventional explanations, I shall not be inserting the word "alleged" before every mention of an encounter. Whatever the cause, these experiences are real, in the sense that they are perceived as such by the majority of those involved. The key issue, of course, is whether or not any of these encounters take place in the physical universe, as opposed to the psychological one." [20]

I think it would be good for US to LOOK into a UFO sighting.

Has anyone seen a UFO?

> Yes, "Seen a UFO) I managed a small advertising channel in the '90s from the local cable television outlet in Grande Prairie, AB. My wife and kids picked me up from work at 5:30. We drove all of half a block when my son noticed a large black triangle in the sky over the GP Inn and said, "Hey look at that

---

20 ARE THEY REALLY HERE? THE UNINVITED. AN EXPOSE OF THE ALIEN ABDUCTION PHENOMENON, Nick Pope.

balloon." It did look pretty unusual, so we pulled into a parking lot and got out of the car for a gander.

It made no noise and had no lights, no exhaust, no smoke and this was in broad daylight. There were three round semi-circles on the bottom, one on each arm of the triangle, and a hole or opening in the middle. It looked to be quite large and didn't drift in the breeze. It was sitting right on the flight path to the airport. We watched it for half an hour to forty-five minutes. Then it just started to climb straight up. It kept that up till it disappeared. Sort of boring really, up till that end part where I got sort of terrified. My wife and kids were beside me.

It was seen by hundreds of people in GP alone. When I got my Alberta Report magazine that month, a business magazine, it turns out that same craft was seen all over Alberta, by thousands of people. It was all over the cover and on the evening news. I have since gone looking for similar craft in reports and that exact same shape has been seen all over the world. If it's one of ours, no one is claiming it. No logos, plain black and not flying, sitting still. Unidentified, flying and an object so... yup, saw one.

It looked just like this one. (not my photo, BTW it took me all of 2 minutes to find a picture of it. Rare eh.)

> *I know the flight controller at the airport, we have played in bands together. So I phoned him when I got home and asked if they had seen 'anything unusual?' I quote, "No one here in the tower saw that giant black triangle Lee. We closed that runway for maintenance. That is our story and we are all sticking to it, pal." I asked what he thought is was and he said, "No clue. We don't make anything that big that will fly. We don't even make anything small that will fly like that."* [21]

It is quite funny. Many people around the world have made reports of seeing a vessel of this nature. They suspect it to be a **(TOP SECRET)** hypersonic aircraft capable of a Mach 6 performance, one that is owned and operated **OCCULTLY** by the United States Air Force or one of their respective intelligence agencies. It is known as the **Aurora / SR-75 Penetrator.**

---

21 https://www.quora.com/Do-UFO-and-aliens-exist-Has-anybody-on-Quora-seen-them-Do-you-have-any-proof?redirected_qid=14534799&share=1 Accessed December 22nd, 2019 @14:43

This image is an artist's impression of the Aurora.[22]

Does the United States Air Force or one of America's intelligence agencies have a secret hypersonic aircraft capable of a Mach 6 performance? According to them no. But do they always tell US the TRUTH? Good question. I will let YOU answer that one.

Please check out the next extract:

> "Continually growing evidence suggests that the answer to this question is yes. Perhaps the most well-known event which provides evidence of such a craft's existence is the sighting of a triangular plane over the North Sea in August 1989 by oil-exploration engineer Chris Gibson. As well as the famous "skyquakes" heard over Los Angeles since the early 1990s, found to be heading for the secret Groom Lake installation in the Nevada desert, numerous *other facts* provide an understanding

---

22 https://www.fighter-planes.com/info/aurora.htm Accessed December 22nd, 2019 @14:39

of how the aircraft's technology works. Rumored to exist but routinely denied by U.S. officials, the name of this aircraft is Aurora. People are also referring to it as the SR-75 Penetrator.

The outside world uses the name Aurora because a censor's slip let it appear below the SR-71 Blackbird and U-2 in the 1985 Pentagon budget request. Even if this was the actual name of the project, it would have by now been changed after being compromised in such a manner. The plane's real name has been kept a secret along with its existence. This is not unfamiliar though, the F-117a stealth fighter was kept a secret for over ten years after its first pre-production test flight. The project is what is technically known as a Special Access Program (SAP). More often, such projects are referred to as "black programs".

So what was the first sign of the existence of such an aircraft? On 6 March 1990, one of the United States Air Force's Lockheed SR-71 Blackbird spy planes shattered the official airspeed record from Los Angeles to Washington's Dulles Airport. There, a brief ceremony marked the end of the SR-71's operational career. Officially, the SR-71 was being retired to save the $200-$300 million a year it cost to operate the fleet. Some reporters were told the plane had been made redundant by sophisticated spy satellites.

But there was one problem, the USAF made no opposition towards the plane's retirement, and congressional attempts to revive the program were discouraged. Never in the history of the USAF had a program been closed without opposition. Aurora is the missing factor to the silent closure of the SR-71 program. Testing such a new radical aircraft brings immense costs and inconvenience, not just in the design and development of a prototype aircraft, but also in providing a secret testing

> *place for aircraft that are obviously different from those the public are aware of.*[23]

One of the most intriguing UFOs ever seen looked just like a flying saucer, as you can see:

Source: [24]

It was the brainchild of scientist Viktor Schauberger. Victor was coerced into working for the NAZI government by Adolf Hitler due to his exceptional knowledge of Pythagoras and Implosion (the utilization of the potential of the inner worlds in the outer world).

The scientific definition of UFO is simply, an object which has a radar reading but refuses to identify itself on the ground or in the air. There have been reports of UFOs throughout the world with more than 70,000 reported cases over the last three

---

23 https://www.fighter-planes.com/info/aurora.htm Accessed December 22nd, 2019 @14:39

24 http://www.illuminati-news.com/00396.html Accessed December 22nd, 2019 @18:14

decades. Many UFO sightings have been written off or explained by other things such as satellites, atmospheric illusions, meteorites, stars, planets, aircrafts, and high altitude weather balloons, etc.

UFOs have been seen and photographed by a whole host of different people, from astronauts, airline pilots, policemen, astronomers, housewives, meteorologists, farmers, people of every race, and religion. They have been photographed with different cameras from polaroid to still, filmed and also tracked by radar. Yet the question remains, DO THEY EXIST?

It is funny when people spot these UFOs their reaction seems genuine in most cases. Genuine shock or excitement of seeing something new, well new to them. But the governments seem to be going on like the old Arsenal manager used to ('Arsene Wenger') – "WE DON'T SEE NOTHING" – "WE DIDN'T SEE ANYTHING." What is wrong with them? They go on as if there has never been any tangible evidence of these flying objects. What have they got to hide?

Nazi Germany was making them during World War Two. The US has been making them quite recently. Russia has been working on hypersonic weapons, crafts, and defense systems for many years now, recently announcing their first regiment of Avangard hypersonic missiles which were put in service at 10:00 Moscow time on 27th December 2019. They are nuclear weapons which have a "glide system" that affords great maneuverability, making them very difficult to defend against. These missiles can travel 20 times the speed of sound and can carry a weight of up to two megatons.[25]

TODAY (to my KNOWLEDGE), Russia aside, not a single country possesses hypersonic weapons or crafts (even though President Trump has been boasting of such things during his recent address on the IRAN situation concerning the assassination of General Soleimani). OUR PLAN-E.T. has had these things before but due to abuse, the materials and KNOWLEDGE were taken away from US. But many countries could be making and testing them secretly for all we know? **These are UFOs.**

Now let us get on to IFOs.

IFOs are Identified Flying Objects. They are UFOs which have been identified, there is not much more I can say really, that is it.

---

[25] https://www.bbc.co.uk/news/amp/world-europe-50927648 Accessed December 29th, 2019 @13:27

I would like you to SEE an article from John Cheshire, a Former Captain, First Officer, and Flight Engineer for several US airlines. He states that throughout four decades of flying he has SEEN just one UNIDENTIFIED FLYING OBJECT; the rest have been IFOs. Please check it out to get the full picture.

> "I saw one (UFO) many years ago. However, before I explain that one sighting, let me preface by saying that over my four decades of flying for both the military and the airlines, I have indeed seen quite a number of Unidentified Flying Objects (UFOs). **Nevertheless, every one of these UFO sighting was soon quickly identified by me or by others later as something easily explainable and mundane, and thus no longer "unidentified"**... except this singular one I now describe:
>
> I was a captain flying a B-737 late at night on a very short leg from Las Vegas (LAS) to Los Angeles (LAX). This was sometime in the 1990s. It was late at night and the more normal heavy air traffic around LAX was greatly reduced at this late hour.
>
> At the time we were early into our descent into LAX via the old Civet Arrival. It was a clear night and a smooth and comfortable flight. Passing through 18,000 feet/5486m we noticed what we thought was another aircraft well off to our left and high above us. We had no other traffic to observe than this one. While we were on perhaps a 30-degree intercept to the final arrival course, this aircraft high and to our left appeared to be on the normal, straight-in course to LAX. We decided this approaching aircraft would not even be close to being a conflict for us since it was well off in the distance. We would intercept

the final inbound course well ahead of him. Since he was not a conflict Approach Control never mentioned him to us either.

Although this traffic off to our left was on the normally expected radial and altitude for the LAX arrival, one thing caught both my First Officer as odd. We were passing below 18,000 feet in our descent. This is the time and altitude that airliners will normally turn on their landing lights for a "see-and-be-seen" standard collision avoidance procedure. However, although this other aircraft was still well above us, he already had all his bright landing lights on. Quietly I wondered to myself why his lights were on so very early. It seemed very odd and I wondered to myself if there was a reason for this.

Switching our radios from Center to LAX Approach Control we turned our attention away from that strange aircraft and concentrated on our approach at hand. Nevertheless, I naturally and briefly glanced a few times at our unusual inbound traffic.

Right before we made the right turn to intercept the final approach course, I once again glanced up at our traffic. What I saw I would never forget! Those bright lights we thought were from an aircraft on approach suddenly and almost instantaneously moved horizontally across the night sky by maybe 35 to 40 degrees and at a considerable distance! Nothing could move that fast! It defied physics. I turned to my First Officer and asked, "Did you see that?" His eyes were as big as saucers as he said, "I sure did!"

There was no craft that I knew of or anything I could ever imagine moving that far and that fast across the sky, and then stopping instantly without any apparent slowing, dead in space. Moreover, no man or beast could ever survive the *amount of G-forces both from that extreme acceleration or the almost instantaneous stop. There was no logical explanation for what we had witnessed. There was even no illogical explanation either. To this day decades later I cannot explain what exactly we saw.*

A few seconds after it had made this astonishing move, it made another much shorter and very quick jump a couple of degrees downward. By this time we were almost passing through the localizer and we had to turn away from this 'thing'. As I looked back over my shoulder I saw it move again horizontally toward its earlier position rapidly, but nowhere near the almost instantaneous movement across the great span we saw earlier. I later wondered if maybe it was the reflection from some kind of searchlight, but it was a clear night with no clouds to reflect upon. Also, it had multiple and distinguishable lights, just like an airliner's.

We never reported this incident although I have thought about it over the years many times. Really what could we say? Besides people look at you funny when you say you "saw something" but don't know what. It also involves a lot of paperwork too, we assumed. So we kept quiet. Curiously I do not even remember my First Officer and I ever talking about it later. It was just one of those unexplained things that we could not explain and did not even want to try.

Ironically the following week I flew the same flight at the same time but we thankfully saw no UFOs this time. What was very curious though was when we switched frequencies, there was a lot of chatter – something unusual for that usually slow time of night. All we could tell from the chatter was that one or more crews "had seen something." There were

> transmissions from several aircraft that said, "Yeah we saw it too." Then Center or Approach came up and asked each aircraft if they wanted to make a report. In rapid sequence, they all said "negative." I never did either.
>
> That's my story and I'm sticking to it!" [26]

I don't know what to THINK, do YOU? It looks like it was a UFO that he saw, maybe it could have been an OOTWFO? Who KNOWS? I don't blame him for not reporting it. We know what happens to people who do - they get silenced, discredited, or deemed mad or crazy. No one is too BIG or small to get 'smoked out' or humiliated as WE can SEE from history.

Did you know that Bobby Kennedy was a firm believer in IFOs? He was a card-carrying member of The Amalgamated Flying Saucer Club of America directed at the time by Gabriel Green a Yucca Valley California contactee. In a letter written to a publisher Gray Barker, Kennedy wrote:

> "Like many other people in our country, I am interested in the UFOs. The prominent Astronomer has stated that there is a probability, that there is life in the universe. I favor more

---

[26] https://www.quora.com/As-a-civil-or-a-military-pilot-have-you-observed-an-object-that-you-believe-to-be-a-UFO-If-so-did-you-report-it-and-what-was-the-response Accessed December 24th, 2019 @07:36

> *research regarding this matter and I hope that once and for all, we can determine the true facts about flying saucers."*

It is said that Kennedy was assassinated because he was too "New Age."[27]

Source: [28]

Many FEEL that that is one of the real reasons why he was assassinated but no one SEEMS to be TALKING about it.

---

27 Man From Planet Rizq, Dr Malachi Z. York, Page 40

28 http://www.openminds.tv/bobby-kennedy-and-ufos/4040 Accessed January 11th, 2020 @21:12

Valiant Thor warned Bobby Kennedy to be careful as there was a plot to kill him. He didn't listen.

Check out the next extract:

> "In a recently rediscovered videotaped interview with Col. Philip J. Corso done by Maurizio Baiata in Rome in July 1997, the colonel reveals that he had personally briefed Attorney General Robert F. Kennedy in the early sixties about the results of his top-secret work of bringing pieces of the Roswell UFO crash to selected companies in the military-industrial complex for developing and adapting the alien technology. You can watch the video clip here. As President Kennedy's younger brother, Bobby Kennedy was not only the Attorney General but also JFK's most trusted advisor. A year after JFK's assassination, he was elected Senator for the state of New York in November 1964, where he soon became a prominent political figure because of his charisma and the Kennedy name. He probably would have become the next president of the United States had he not been murdered during the celebration of his victory of the California primary at The Ambassador Hotel in Los Angeles, just after midnight on June 5, 1968.
>
> We only have Corso's testimony for his briefing, so we made a thorough search of the public record to see if there were any clues about Bobby Kennedy and the UFO subject. Ironically, the best-known document where he expresses a strong belief in UFOs—a letter to ufologist Gray Barker dated May 9, 1968—may be a forgery. We'll discuss our research into this letter later on, but let's look first at other letters written by Sen. Kennedy in the 1965-1966 period. Until recently, only the Barker letter and a couple of brief responses sent by Sen. Kennedy to Robert

Barrow, were available. John Greenwald of www.blackvault.com, however, obtained a dossier of 127 pages from the Kennedy presidential library which gives a far more complete picture of the NY senator's involvement with UFOs. The letters cover a period between 1965 and 1968 and contain 39 letters signed by Kennedy himself, plus the original letters he received from a number of constituents and UFO researchers, U.S. Air Force statements, some newspaper clippings, etc.

The period of 1965 and 1966 was the most active in Bobby Kennedy's UFO correspondence. This coincided with a lobbying effort by the National Investigation Committee on Aerial Phenomena (NICAP) to have Congressional hearings on UFOs. NICAP was then the nation's most influential UFO group led by the late Major (Ret.) Donald Keyhoe in the Washington, DC area. Out of the 27 individuals who wrote to Kennedy, most belonged to NICAP and some, like Robert Barrow, Raymond Konley, and Ralph Rankow, wrote several letters to him. I was also surprised to see many names who were relatively well known in the UFO field—some of whom I knew personally—including the contactee Wayne Aho, the aviation journalist Don Berliner, the Rev. Frank Stranges, John Keel, author of The Mothman Prophecies *and other important UFO and Fortean books, and the psychic Ted Owens, among others. When I saw the name of Terry Wilmot with an address in Roswell, NM, the name rang a bell. He was, in fact, the son of Dan Wilmot, who reported with his wife a UFO-shaped "like two invert saucers faced mouth-to-mouth" on the night of July 2, 1947, shortly before the famous crash. His sighting was published in the Roswell Daily Record, although it's not mentioned in Terry's letter to Bobby Kennedy (Terry, too, was a member of NICAP).*

Back in the 1960s, form letters had not been developed to the exact science than they are today, so Bobby Kennedy's letters vary a little from one to the other, but some general themes nevertheless emerge clearly. He is, of course, a polished politician, always polite to his constituents, thanking them "for your thoughtful letter," appreciating them for "your thoughtfulness in writing to me on this matter," and so on. He then tries to walk a thin line between appearing open-minded enough while at the same time making it clear that, "from the evidence available to date, I do not believe that UFO phenomena are caused by vehicles of extraterrestrial origin." Here is a typical response, in this case to Terry Wilmot of Roswell, NM, dated April 11, 1965:" [29]

---

[29] http://www.openminds.tv/bobby-kennedy-and-ufos/4040 Accessed January 11th, 2020 @17:28

Choices 2

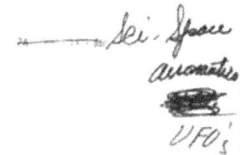

August 11, 1965

Mr. Terry M. Wilmot
1808 West Fourth Street
Roswell, New Mexico 88201

Dear Mr. Wilmot:

    Thank you for your letter asking my views concerning so-called UFO's or unidentified flying objects.

    I have noted from time to time public discussions about UFO's and the bases for such phenomena. From the evidence available to date, I do not believe that UFO phenomena are caused by vehicles of extraterrestrial origin.

    However, scientists agree that not enough is known about UFO sightings, in some cases by reputable witnesses, to definitely identify the cause of the phenomena. I hope that science can provide us with an answer to these unknown aspects of UFO sightings.

Source: [30]

---

[30] http://www.openminds.tv/bobby-kennedy-and-ufos/4040 Accessed January 11th, 2020 @17:28

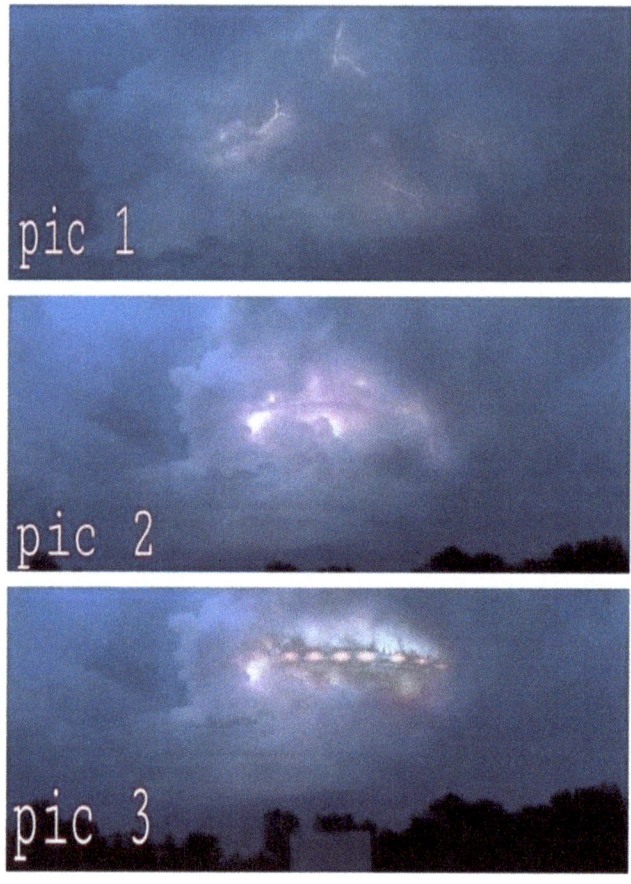

Source: 31

Is this an OOTWFO?

Apparently so. What about the Gulf Breeze sightings:

---

31 https://www.facebook.com/photo.php?fbid=10203154538496051&set=gm
.774434669277416&type=3&theater Accessed December 23rd, 2019 @ 09:00

Choices 2

Source:[32]

> "The overwhelming evidence is in. Gulf Breeze is indeed one of the most incredible cases in modern UFO history."[33]

---

32 https://seanmunger.com/2014/02/01/fake-me-to-your-leader-the-great-gulf-breeze-ufo-hoax/ Accessed January 11th, 2020 @18:11

This is one of the most notorious UFO sightings in history. Between 1987 and 1993 in the Gulf Breeze, a small city in Florida of approximately 6000 people, there had been many reports of UFO sightings, photographs, and videos, beginning in the winter of 1987.

Please check out the next extract:

> "Of the many accounts of UFO sightings, photographs, and videos, the sensational reports that originated in Gulf Breeze, Florida are some of the most controversial. Gulf Breeze was a small city of approximately 6,000 at the time of the wave of sightings that began in the winter of 1987.
>
> News of UFO photos par excellence spread rapidly and far, becoming a worldwide sensation, and the subject of a plethora of newspaper and magazine articles, television talk shows, and feature programs.
>
> Though many sighted the elusive flying craft and snapped photographs of the glowing lights, the majority of attention was on one Edward Walters, a local building contractor. According to Walters, the sightings began on November 11, 1987. He was working late that night when his attention was drawn to a light coming from his yard.
>
> As he went to the window to get a better vantage point, he saw a glowing object partially obscured by a 30-foot tall pine

---

33 https://ufocasebook.com/gulfbreeze.html Accessed January 11th, 2020 @18:07

tree in his front yard. Racing outside to get a clearer view of the object, he was taken back by the sight before him. He was staring at an object with the shape of a top.

It had a row of dark squares which were separated with portals between them. The craft seemed to hover just above the road, showing a glowing ring around its bottom. Ed ran into his house and grabbed his Polaroid camera. He snapped off several photos of the craft before deciding to get even closer. He headed into the road.

As he paused in the street to take more photos of the strange object, it began to hover almost directly over his head. Walters was then hit by a bright bluish beam which shot from the object. He was literally lifted from the ground by its force. It was then that he heard a voice say, "Don't worry, we will not harm you." Images began to enter his mind.

Ed stated the images were revealed to him "as if they were turning the pages of a book" The next thing Walters remembered was waking up. The glowing UFO was nowhere to be seen.

Only a few days later, on November 17, Walters took his photographs and story to the local Gulf Breeze Sentinel newspaper. Ed discussed the photographs with the paper's editor and began to relate to him the details of the sighting.[34]

I have left a footnote at the bottom of the page to the full article.

So many people have seen this UFO, it was a major sensation at the time. I am not sure about Ed Walters as I was not there at the time. But what I do know, however, is that the media and government tried to discredit him. But again, that is nothing new.

This is Wikipedia's take on it:

> "Gulf Breeze UFO Incident
>
> **The Gulf Breeze UFO incident** was a series of claimed UFO sightings in Gulf Breeze Florida during 1987.
>
> **History**
>
> Beginning in November 1987, The Gulf Breeze Sentinel published a number of photos supplied to them by local contractor Ed Walters that were claimed to show a UFO. UFOlogists such as Bruce Maccabee believed the photographs were genuine, however, others strongly suspected them to be a hoax. Pensacola News Journal reporter Craig Myers investigated Walters' claims a few years later, criticizing the

---

34 https://ufocasebook.com/gulfbreeze.html Accessed January 11th, 2020 @18:04

Sentinel's coverage of the story as "uncritical" and "sensationalist". Myers was able to duplicate Walters's UFO photos almost exactly using a styrofoam model UFO found in the attic of the house where Walters had been living at the time the photos were published.

Please check out this next extract, it fills in a few more gaps. I will leave a link to the full article at the bottom of the page:

> "The videotape from Ed was also scrutinized by UFO experts. Bob Oescheler observed the video and determined that it was a flying craft that was not operated by remote control. Bruce McAbee determined that the object was twelve feet wide and nine feet tall. Skeptics suggest that the UFOs are actually military aircraft being tested at the nearby Pensacola Naval Air Station. However, the military has denied any involvement in the sightings, claiming that they do not have aircraft that match the description of the objects.
>
> **Extra notes:** The case was featured as a part of the October 5, 1988 episode. A significant update to this story aired on October 3, 1990. Due to the controversy surrounding the sightings, Ed Walters used the fictitious name "Ray" and was not interviewed on camera during the original segment. Fenner McConnell was killed in a hit & run accident while riding his bike July 5th, 1998; he was 63. The driver who struck McConnell turned himself several hours later after seeing on the local news that McConnell had been killed.

Results: Unresolved. In December of 1988, Ed Walters and his family moved out of their house in Gulf Breeze. Ten months later, the house was purchased by Bob and Sara Lee Menzer. In March of 1990, Bob went into the attic to look for a shutoff valve for the water pipes. While searching through the insulation, he found a model of a UFO. At the time, they did not realize the importance of it, as they had not heard about the sightings beforehand.

Two months later in June, a reporter met with the Menzers and asked them about the sightings. He also asked if they had found anything associated with UFOs in the home. At that point, they recalled the model that they had found in the attic. They brought the model to the reporter, who took it to the offices of his newspaper. The following week, the story of the model's discovery made headlines in Gulf Breeze. Ed, however, claimed that someone had planted the model in order to discredit him. The Pensacola paper showed how the model could be used in a hoax. Reporter Mark Curtis believes that the model is quite similar to the object seen in Ed's photos. He suspects that a similar model was used to make the alleged hoax photos. The model is 9 inches across and 6 inches high. The black porthole are drawn on a strip of drafting paper cut *from one of Ed's discarded house designs. According to Ed, however, his plan was made in September of 1989, almost two years after his initial photographs. Also, the witnesses from the sightings are certain that what they saw was not a model in the sky.*

Gulf Breeze mayor Ed Gray believes that the photos were a hoax, created so that Ed Walters could make money and publicity off of them. Although many became convinced that the photos and sightings were hoaxes, others still believed in him. In fact, during a more recent sighting when Ed took new photographs of another object, there were other witnesses with him.

In January of 1989, he and his wife were walking in their neighborhood when they noticed a red object in the sky. They returned home and called Duane Cook, telling him to come quickly. Moments later, Ed was joined by Brenda and Buddy Pollack, along with Duane and his family. They all saw a red object in the sky. However, the object looked much different than the objects previously photographed by him. After the object disappeared, Brenda took a time exposure photograph of the sky. The object appeared as a long string of colors. Experts determined that it had made over one-hundred color changes in the three-second exposure. This incident was only the second time that someone other than an immediate family member had seen Ed photograph a UFO. While this seemed to give credibility to Ed and his photographs, other witnesses later emerged that suggested it was a hoax after all. One week after the model was discovered, twenty-year-old Gulf Breeze resident Tommy Smith came forward. He claimed that Ed had asked him to help create the hoax photographs. In January of 1988, Ed gave him six photos and told him to take them to the local papers. However, he did not go through with it. For two years, he kept this information secret from everyone except his parents. However, he said that he came forward because the model would help show that his story was the truth. Ed, of course, claimed that Tommy was lying.

In another newscast, Mark Curtis helped show how one of the photographs (where the UFO appeared to be landing on the road) could have been faked. UFO researcher Jerry Black later discovered a suspicious trail of money that led to Ed Walters, giving indications of a hoax. However, the UFO sightings in Gulf Breeze have never been completely explained." 35

To this day, there is so much confusion concerning this particular UFO. Why? Because it is an OOTWFO (Out of This World Flying Object)! The government approach was also very strange, but I am not surprised. I guess they are not used to dealing with communicating to US about stolen shams but that is another story. But what actually do OUR GOVERNMENTS and ARMED FORCES **DISCLOSE** to US?

---

35 https://unsolvedmysteries.fandom.com/wiki/Gulf_Breeze_UFO Accessed November 11th, 2020 @18:29

Choices 2

Source: 36

Look at the photos and video footage at the links below:

https://www.express.co.uk/news/weird/891346/World-best-UFO-picture-Gulf-Breeze-UFO-Florida-proof-aliens

https://www.youtube.com/watch?v=e4o5IZUHTiQ

I will let you make YOUR OWN MIND UP.

OOTWFOs are **Out of This World Flying Objects.** Around 90% of UFO sightings become recognized as IFOs at some point, which would leave 10% of the sightings as an anomaly. **In this case, WE need to ASK:** Are these FLYING OBJECTS from this world or are they from another world? If

---

36 https://www.express.co.uk/news/weird/891346/World-best-UFO-picture-Gulf-Breeze-UFO-Florida-proof-aliens Accessed November 11th, 2020 @18:42

the OBJECT in QUESTION was from this WORLD we would need to KNOW first, if it were from INNER or OUTER EARTH, and secondly, if it is an occult (BLACK OPS) vehicle from another country. What are YOUR THOUGHTS on this?

Do you MIND if I ask you something? How much do WE KNOW about CLOUDS? What are CLOUDS? Are they USED as covers for vehicles not native to this PLAN-E.T. to hide the extra-terrestrial PHENOMENA from US? Don't MIND me I was just SPEAKING OUT, just throwing some THOUGHTS in the AIR, who KNOWS? Do YOU? And what about the chemtrails. What are they? What I do KNOW is that most of what WE have been TAUGHT in this LIFE has been so untrue. Everything seems to have a REAL STORY behind it or an AGENDA which is often initially HIDDEN. WHY is THIS? It sure gets one THINKING.

ONE UNDENIABLE FACT and DIVINE TRUTH is that LIFE beyond this EARTH does exist. Do YOU REALLY THINK that WE are the ONLY LIFE out of TRILLIONS of STARS and PLANETS in the MULTIVERSE?

REALLY?

WHAT IS LIFE?

I started this chapter talking about aliens and extra-terrestrials questioning whether they exist or not. I have my own thoughts about this subject area, I am sure that you have yours too. I would like to finish off this chapter with an extract from my good brother Sean Pereira, he always has something interesting to say:

> "Remember ALI.EN. "EXTRA TERRASTRAL."
>
> "Get Ready for Major UFO or IFO (IDENTIFIED FLYING OBJECTS sightings"
>
> An EXTRA- TERRESTRIAL is a being not from Earth, that was born and lived on another planet, another solar system, another Galaxy.
>
> An INNER-TERRESTRIAL can be a being that resides in another dimension yet that dimension seems to be located inside the earth like Shambhala, the capital city of AGARTHA.
>
> NIVARNA is a state of conscious yet a physical plane in ORION.
>
> The Hindus have always claimed that they came to earth in VIMINAAS or flying crafts.
>
> The DOGONS in Africa have documented proof of their SIRIUS Connection.

The GODS AND ANGELS of all religions are EXTRATERRASTRAL = EXTRA on earth from ASTRAL, the stars.

The natives of AMERICA have always handed down oral stories about the THUNDERBIRDS, THE KACHINAS, and the HOPI here in Arizona has made it clear that KOKOPELLI Koko is coco or dark brown, and PELE is GOD, or BLACK GOD a MOOR from outer space.

Many people on earth are channeling different species of extra-terrestrials at the RISK of sounding crazy and being from RIZQ, and it's not a SHAM, the crafts of the RIZQIANS are called SHAMS. MALACHI Z. YORK has declared that he is the incarnation of an EXTRATERRASTRAL called TEHUTI, " YANAAN". An intergalactic traveler, and teacher from the 8 the planet "RIZQ" (marzaq) in the 19th GALAXY ILLYUWN. Speaks 19 languages retranslated all the scriptures and revealed one he wrote called the HOLY TABLETS, yet he is not given proper credit in the mainstream media, they seek to destroy his credibility and now he is Imprisoned in Colorado super max. Yet unstoppable.

So we have DISCLOSURE, and proof that EXTRA TERRA ASTRALS are real.

"We Are Not Alone."

Shawn Pereira, December 1, 2018 (The Re Turn Council Of The All Expanding.)[37]

After reading this, I would like to ask you once again, What are your THOUGHTS about all of this?

I am sorry that this chapter is a little long, there has just been so much to cover. I would have loved to have gone more in-depth but it would have taken a whole book at the very least.

Before and after reading this I am not sure how you THINK and FEEL about UFOs, IFOs, and OOTWFOs. To me, it is gleamingly obvious that **all** such things exist. The evidence

---

37 https://www.facebook.com/permalink.php?story_fbid=2096860093961517&id=100009126390100 Accessed January 12th, 2020 @06:40

and reports of millions of people worldwide seem to back up my comments.

The GOVERNMENTS and their CONTROLLERS also give the GAME away. Why else would people get threatened, hushed up, or smoked out when they tell the truth about what they see? And why do they always cover up sightings and reports? Why are some sworn to secrecy? Why do governments and their financiers, for the most part, deny the existence of UFOs, IFOs, and OOTWFOs? Why do governments and their financiers deny the existence of these secret black operation projects (that always burn through millions of taxpayers' money each time)? Maybe they have something to hide? Maybe they are more worried than US?

Can you IMAGINE running a PLAN-E.T. experiencing extra-terrestrial and inner-terrestrial beings and crafts coming and going as they please? Ones with far greater technology, speeds, and greater capabilities? Can you IMAGINE these beings, they come, abduct the people of your PLAN-E.T. as they please? And when you get your armed FORCES out to deal with these RETRABATES, you get outfoxed, outmaneuvered, and outgunned every time? You cannot catch them or blow them up, but they let you see them sometimes? They give you warnings through good citizens to stop playing with all your dangerous weapons, but you do not listen. You try to catch them instead to blow them up with your best, most advanced supersonic weapons only to be eluded on almost every single occasion.

In the past, they had trusted you, made deals with you, and helped you in exchange for technology but you broke all agreements and reneged on all deals. Now YOUR citizens are BACKWARDS and STUPID, they have not LEARNED and DEVELOPED from their PAST MASTERS, much OLD KNOWLEDGE has been LOST. You do not even know about the ART of LEVITATION, about TIME TRAVEL or MAGNETISM. You are not skilled in IMPLOSION. You do not bother with the higher senses when they are the main ones???

The technology that was given to you, you used for destructive purposes against **NATURE** - the nature of this PLAN-E.T. and others throughout the multiverse. This is why they will not help you anymore until you blow yourself up and destroy the PLAN-E.T. or until NATURAL ORDER is RESTORED on YOUR PLAN-E.T. EARTH (GAIA). There is nothing that you can do against these superior beings and you KNOW it. They have access to around 600 elements, which can build advanced technology with insurmountable capabilities, whereas YOU barely have over 99.

YOU are more SCARED than the citizens that have nominated you to REPRESENT them. IMAGINE if they FOUND OUT WHAT HAD BEEN GOING ON ALL THESE YEARS? IMAGINE IF THEY FOUND OUT THAT YOU WERE ALSO ALIENS (WHO HAVE SICK FETISHES)? Can YOU IMAGINE the WORLD'S ACTIONS when they FIND OUT? It would spread mass PANIC! NATURALLY.

I wonder if they know that STAR WARS was based on a real story and is not just a make-believe MOVIE? But as they SAY:

"Everyone needs to be responsible for their own actions".

YOUR TIME IS OVER AND YOU KNOW IT!

I don't KNOW how YOU FEEL but I would never like to be in this position. What are YOUR THOUGHTS?

Some people think that seeing is believing, some people always need social proof. But that is silly if you ask me? WIND exists. WE KNOW THIS! Can we SEE it BLOW? Exactly. Do YOU get the POINT?

There is always so much that WE CANNOT SEE, which is THERE – PRESENT. WE really should be asking OURSELVES, WHAT CAN WE SEE. Most people CANNOT SEE a lot. Most of US have three eyes but only generally work with two, which doesn't make sense. Why neglect or forget about our most important eye? Why? I will tell you - LACK of KNOWLEDGE. I am going to tell you this FACT whether you believe me or not, but WE would actually SEE more if WE were BLIND as WE would be WORKING with OUR most IMPORTANT EYE, OUR INTERNAL EYE, OUR SPIRITUAL EYE, OUR THIRD EYE. Don't just believe me, please check it out for yourself.

Do OOTWFOs exist? Can WE prove it or not? Very good question if you ask me. We have ancient cave paintings around the world today which depict different UFO looking crafts with strange alien-looking beings (strange to us). Of course, WE have classified vehicles and craft, which are often misperceived or misidentified as OOTWFOs such as the F-117 stealth fighter, the SR-71 Blackbird spy plane, the flying saucer, the Aurora/SR-75 Penetrator, etc. Of course, WE have space debris, comets, meteorites which can be seen traveling at tremendous speeds, but this does not explain the sightings that cannot be explained (which happens) in around 10% of the cases? UKNOWN, UNEXPLAINED vehicles and craft have been doing some pretty abnormal stuff in OUR airspaces, yet WE KNOW NOTHING. WE ARE KEPT in the DARK. SURELY SOMEBODY KNOWS SOMETHING? WHY are they not SAYING anything to US? The only thing that we get is a little bit of SOFT DISCLOSURE, here and there. I wonder WHY?

Quite recently three videos were released, taken by F-18 gun cameras which showed a craft that had been following a number of our naval carrier groups. This craft, which was tracked on radar by several vessels, went from zero to thousands of miles per hour instantly. It was the Pentagon itself that declared the videos to be authentically authorizing that they could be released to the general public. This is SOFT DISCLOSURE; we will touch on this more in the next chapter.

CHAPTER 7B
DISCLOSURE

Why would anyone want to tell the truth in this day and age? And who would they tell it too? If I was running around telling people that I had seen an INNER TERRAASTRAL or EXTRATERRASTRAL or an OOTWFO, people would THINK that I was out of MIND, can you IMAGINE? I would get more results if I told them that SANTA or the TOOTH FAIRY are real or if I said that Jesus was coming back. If I did SEE such a PHENOMENA for REAL, who could I REALISTICALLY TELL? WHAT WOULD HAPPEN TO ME IF I REPORTED IT TO THE MEDIA or the POLICE? I wouldn't LIKE to IMAGINE. CAN YOU? They would probably send the Men in Black after me. You don't think they are a fairytale do you or something that is just in a movie? This life is funny, strange, and mysterious.

CAN YOU SEE WHERE WE ARE AT? Just look at JFK, RFK, MLK, Bob Marley, Prodigy, Tupac, John Lennon, Bill

Cosby, Princess Diana, and Malachi Z. York. THEY ALL DISCLOSED TRUTHS AND LOOK WHAT HAPPENED TO THEM? Malachi Z. York EXPOSED so MANY TRUTHS, LOOK what happened to him. Imprisoned for 135 years on FALSE ALLEGATIONS, INCARCERATED without any EVIDENCE being held against him? His trial took place on a PUBLIC HOLIDAY. A closed court with sealed TRANSCRIPTS and that is not even touching the surface. How many GOOD/POSITIVE people have to go before WE get the GAME that is being PLAYED on US???

Disclosure, such a funny thing, in this day and age. Why would anyone do it KNOWING the CONSEQUENCES? I am speaking from a hypothetical view here. But the QUESTION still STANDS.

QUESTION: DISCLOSURE - Why would anyone do it **KNOWING** the CONSEQUENCES?

ANSWER: DIVINE LOVE

Some of US NEED to have it OTHERWISE this WORLD WOULD END, we couldn't have that, could WE? It is TRUE, this PLAN.E.T. has been RUN by PSYCHOPATHS for THOUSANDS of years, some of them are Satanists, whilst the others are Luciferian, but their **TIME** is **OVER NOW** and I am very happy. **WE ALL NEED** to **NOTICE** and **REALIZE**.

NOW WE LIVE IN A TIME WHEN THERE CAN BE NO MORE SECRETS. KNOWLEDGE IS POWER, DIVINE LOVE IS EVERYTHING. WE ARE ALL PART OF THE ALL AND WE ALL HAVE A PART TO PLAY. EVEN IF IT IS JUST TO BE WIPED OUT, CLEANSING, IN ANY CASE, NEEDS TO HAPPEN. NATURE DOES HAVE A KNACK OF NATURALLY SORTING THESE THINGS OUT.

LIKE ATTRACTS LIKE – WE KNOW THIS. POSITIVE BEINGS ATTRACT OTHER POSITIVE BEINGS and VICE VERSA. SIT on THE FENCE BEINGS WILL ATTRACT OTHER SIT ON THE FENCE BEINGS. THIS is MAGNETISM, a MAJOR FORCE in this MULTIVERSE. WITHOUT MAGNETISM, WHERE WOULD WE BE? And what about ALL the PLAN-E.T.'S. How would they be all locked into orbit? THIS is NATURAL ORDER, if YOU HAVE PATIENCE and TAKE TIME OBSERVE, you will SEE IT.

WE ALL HAVE FREE WILL, WE ALL HAVE CHOICE, WE DECIDE. WE CAN ALL WALK IN THE LIGHT, IN TRUTH IN LOVE or WE CAN PERISH. **A NEW GOLDEN AGE IS JUST BEGINNING! MARK MY WORDS!**

Please check out the next extract, it kind of fits into what we are discussing here:

> "In 1952 we had overflights above the Capitol building by a fleet of around 30 saucer-shaped craft on two consecutive weekends. The official govt response was a temperature inversion though multiple radar operators knew that explanation was a lie but they were not allowed to say so in public - however, one of the operators told a famous UFO investigator the truth shortly before he died around the year 2000.
>
> So we have already had something akin to a UFO landing on the Whitehouse lawn, but the press, infiltrated by the CIA (Project MOCKINGBIRD), willfully accepted the government's obvious lie to maintain the UFO coverup which had been in place from 1947 to 2018, when the US Navy officially acknowledged the existence of UFOs by officially releasing three gun camera video's made by F-18's which had encountered a TicTac shaped craft that had entered a battlegroup's air space multiple times, off the coast of California, in 2004.
>
> The TicTac craft performed maneuvers completely impossible to any known aircraft at the time. Its maneuvers suggested the craft had inertial mass canceling technology as the G forces generated by said maneuvers would have killed any human who happened to be inside. The exterior of the craft was perfectly smooth, with no visible exhaust outlets, which also suggests some type of gravity manipulation technology, using a means of Propulsion unavailable to publicly known technology."

Choices 2

I am not sure what happened here? A fleet of around thirty saucer shape crafts is a little different from one TicTac craft, don't you think? What is going on? I am sure you get my point. Our governments and their shadow controllers only disclose TRUTHS to US if it's beneficial to them or if their hands are forced. In instances like this, they usually try to get away with a little bit of SOFT DISCLOSURE like the above example.

I am very sorry this is going to be another long chapter, please stay with me. I would like you to read the extract below as it contains some very interesting and important information, which may be new to YOU. I will leave a link to the full article in the footnotes, please check it out if you can.

Milton William "Bill" Cooper was an American conspiracy theorist, radio broadcaster, and author best known for his 1991 book Behold a Pale Horse, in which he warned of multiple global conspiracies, some involving extra-terrestrial life. Bill Cooper was born into a military family, he grew up in bases all over the world, eventually becoming attached to naval intelligence. His father was USAF Lt. Col. (Ret) Milton V Cooper. Bill Cooper felt extremely betrayed by the government he once served for many years to protect the country he loved. He was assassinated on November 5, 2001 (killed in a confrontation with police at The **Cooper** Ranch).

Kwadwo Naya: Baa Ankh Em Ra A'lyun Eil

Please check out the article below it is quite long but very interesting:

A Covenant with Death by Milton William Cooper

(Posted by Wes Penre, May 2, 2005)

The following document was released by William Cooper to members of various UFO RESEARCH and PATRIOT RESEARCH organizations. The manuscript, which ties together certain aspects of the "Secret Government" and the "UFO Phenomena", was titled: THE SECRET GOVERNMENT (The Origin, Identity, and Purpose of MJ-12. May 23, 1989. Updated November 21, 1990):

"...I originally wrote this piece as a research paper. It was first delivered at the MUFON Symposium on July 2, 1989, in Las Vegas, Nevada. Most of this knowledge comes directly from or as a result of my own research into the TOP SECRET/MAJIC material WHICH I SAW AND READ between the years 1970 and 1973 as a member of the Intelligence Briefing Team of the Commander in Chief of the Pacific Fleet. Since some of this information was derived from sources that I cannot divulge for obvious reasons, and from published sources which I cannot vouch for...(this) must be termed a hypothesis. I firmly believe that if the aliens are real, THIS IS THE TRUE NATURE OF THE BEAST. It is the only scenario THAT ANSWERS ALL THE QUESTIONS and places the various fundamental mysteries in an arena that makes sense. It is the only explanation that shows the chronology of events and demonstrates that the chronologies, when assembled, match perfectly. The bulk of this I believe to be true if the material that I viewed in the Navy is authentic.

As for the rest, I do not know, and that is why this paper must be termed a hypothesis. Most historic and currently available evidence supports this hypothesis.

During the years following World War II, the government of the United States was confronted with a series of events which were to change beyond prediction its future and with it the future of humanity. These events were so incredible that they defied belief. A stunned President Truman and his top military commanders found themselves virtually impotent after having just won the most devastating and costly war in history.

The United States had developed, used, and was the only nation on earth in possession of the atomic bomb. This new weapon had the potential to destroy an enemy, and even the Earth itself. At that time the United States had the best economy, the most advanced technology, the highest standard of living, exerted the most influence, and fielded the largest and most powerful military forces in history. We can only imagine the confusion and concern when the informed elite of the United States Government discovered that an alien spacecraft piloted by 'insect like' beings from a totally incomprehensible culture had crashed in the desert of New Mexico (Note: Some have alleged that certain 'sauroids' appear 'insect-like'. Other indications suggest that they may be 'para-physical' entities of some sort, perhaps those allegedly released, according to Kenneth Grant and others, by the Illuminati from another 'dimension' via holes torn in the space-time fabric by the early atomic tests in the Nevada underground, New Mexico, and elsewhere - Branton).

Between January 1947 and December 1952, at

least 16 crashed or downed alien craft, 65 bodies, and 1 live alien were recovered. An additional alien craft had exploded, and nothing was recovered from that incident. Of these events, 13 occurred within the borders of the United States, not including the craft which disintegrated in the air. Of these 13, 1 was in Arizona, 11 were in New Mexico, and 1 was in Nevada. Sightings of UFOs were so numerous that serious investigation and debunking of each report became impossible, utilizing the existing intelligence assets.

An alien craft was found on February 13, 1948, on a mesa near Aztec, New Mexico. Another craft was located on March 25, 1948, in White Sands Proving Ground. It was 100 feet in diameter. A total of 17 alien bodies were recovered from those two crafts. Of even greater significance was the discovery of a large number of human body parts stored within both of these vehicles. A demon had reared its head and paranoia quickly took hold of everyone 'in the know.' The Secret lid immediately became a Top-Secret lid and was screwed down tight. THE SECURITY BLANKET WAS EVEN TIGHTER THAN THAT IMPOSED UPON THE MANHATTAN PROJECT. In the coming years, these events were to become the most closely guarded secrets in the history of the world.

A special group of America's top scientists was organized under the name Project SIGN in December 1947 to study the phenomena. The whole nasty business was contained. Project SIGN evolved into Project GRUDGE in December 1948. A low-level collection and disinformation project named BLUE BOOK was formed under GRUDGE. Sixteen volumes were to come out of GRUDGE. "Blue Teams" were put together to recover the crashed disks or live aliens. The Blue Teams were later to evolve into Alpha Teams under Project POUNCE.

DURING THESE EARLY YEARS THE UNITED STATES AIR FORCE AND THE CENTRAL INTELLIGENCE AGENCY EXERCISED COMPLETE CONTROL OVER THE 'ALIEN SECRET.' In fact, the CIA was formed by Presidential Executive Order first as the Central Intelligence Group for the express purpose of dealing with the alien presence. Later the National Security Act was passed, establishing it as the Central Intelligence Agency.

The National Security Council was established to oversee the intelligence community and especially the alien endeavor. A series of National Security Council memos and Executive orders removed the CIA from the sole task of gathering foreign intelligence and slowly but thoroughly 'legalized' direct action in the form of covert activities at home and abroad.

On December 9, 1947, Truman approved the issuance of NSC-4, entitled 'Coordination of Foreign Intelligence Information Measures' at the urging of the Secretaries Marshall, Forrestal, Patterson, and the director of the State Department's Policy Planning Staff, George Kennan.

The FOREIGN AND MILITARY INTELLIGENCE, BOOK I, 'Final Report of the Select Committee to Study Governmental Operations with respect to Intelligence Activities,' United States Senate, 94th Congress, 2nd Session, Report No. 94-755, April 26, 1976, p. 49. states: 'This directive empowered the Secretary to coordinate overseas information activities designed to counter communism.'

A Top Secret annex to NSC-4, NSC-4A, instructed the director of Central Intelligence to undertake covert psychological activities in pursuit of the aims outlined in NSC-4. The initial authority given the CIA for covert operations under NSC-4A did not establish formal procedures for either coordinating or approving these operations. It simply directed the DCI to 'undertake covert actions and to ensure, through liaison with Senate and Defense, that the resulting operations were consistent with American policy.'

Later NSC-10/1 and NSC-10/2 were to supersede NSC-4 and NSC-4A and expand the covert abilities even further. The Office of Policy Coordination (OPC) was chartered to carry out an expanded program of covert activities. NSC-10/1 and NSC-10/2 validated illegal and extra-legal practices and procedures as being agreeable to the national security leadership. The reaction was swift. In the eyes of the intelligence community, 'no holds were barred.' Under NSC-10/1 an Executive Coordination Group was established to review, but not approve, covert project proposals. The ECG was secretly tasked to coordinate the alien projects. NSC-10/1 & /2 were interpreted to mean that no one at the top wanted to know about anything until it was over and successful.

These actions established a buffer between the President and the information. It was intended that this buffer serves as a means for the President to deny knowledge if leaks divulged the true state of affairs. This buffer was used in later years to effectively isolate succeeding Presidents from any knowledge of the alien presence OTHER THAN WHAT THE SECRET GOVERNMENT AND THE INTELLIGENCE COMMUNITY WANTED THEM TO KNOW. NSC-10/2 established a study panel that met secretly and was made up of the scientific minds of the day. The study panel was not called MJ-12. Another NSC memo, NSC-10/5 further outlined the duties of the study panel. These NSC memos and secret

Executive orders SET THE STAGE FOR THE CREATION OF MJ-12 ONLY FOUR YEARS LATER.

SECRETARY OF DEFENSE JAMES FORRESTAL OBJECTED TO THE SECRECY. *He was a very idealistic and religious man. He believed that the public should be told. James Forrestal was also one of the first known abductees. When he began to talk to leaders of the opposition party and leaders of the Congress about the alien problem he was asked to resign by Truman. He expressed his fears to many people. Rightfully, he believed that he was being watched. This was interpreted by those who were ignorant of the facts as paranoia. Forrestal later was said to have suffered a mental breakdown. He was ordered to the mental ward of Bethesda Naval Hospital. Even though* THE ADMINISTRATION HAD NO AUTHORITY TO HAVE HIM COMMITTED, *the order was carried out. It was feared that Forrestal would begin to talk again. He had to be isolated and discredited. His family and friends were denied permission to visit. Finally, on May 21, 1949, Forrestal's brother made a fateful decision.* HE NOTIFIED AUTHORITIES THAT HE INTENDED TO REMOVE JAMES FROM BETHESDA *on May 22. Sometime in the early morning of May 22, 1949, agents of the CIA tied a sheet around James Forrestal's neck, fastened the other end to a fixture in his room, then threw James Forrestal out the window. The sheet tore and he plummeted to his death. James Forrestal's secret diaries were confiscated by the CIA and were kept in the White House for many years. Due to public demand, the diaries were eventually rewritten and published in a sanitized version. The real diary information was later furnished by the CIA in book form to an agent who published the material as fiction.* THE NAME OF THE AGENT IS WHITLEY STRIEBER *and the book is*

'MAJESTIC'. James Forrestal became one of the first victims of the cover-up.

The live alien that had been found wandering in the desert from the 1949 Roswell crash was named EBE. The name had been suggested by Vannevar Bush and was short for Extra-terrestrial Biological Entity. EBE HAD A TENDENCY TO LIE, and for over, a year would give only the desired answer to questions asked. Those questions which would have resulted in an undesirable answer went unanswered. At one point during the second year of captivity, he began to open up. The information derived from EBE was startling, to say the least. This compilation of his revelations became the foundation of what would later be called the 'Yellow Book.' Photographs were taken of EBE which, among others, I was to view years later in Project Grudge.

In late 1951 EBE became ill. Medical personnel had been unable to determine the cause of EBE's illness and had no background from which to draw... Several experts were called in to study the illness. These specialists included medical doctors, botanists, and entomologists. A botanist, Guillermo Mendoza, was brought in to try and help him recover. Mendoza worked to save EBE until June 2, 1952, when EBE died. Mendoza became the expert on at least this type of alien biology. The movie E.T. is the thinly disguised story of EBE.

In a futile attempt to save EBE and to gain favor with this technologically superior race, the United States began broadcasting a call for help *early in 1952 into the vast regions of space. The call went unanswered but the project, dubbed SIGMA, continued as an effort of good faith (Note: Apparently in this effort to kiss-up to a more technically advanced race of creatures these government officials forgot EBE's infernal "tendency to lie", and instead continued to believe what they WANTED to believe that this was a sure way to satisfy their insatiable appetite for super technology and that these creatures were benevolent - even though human body parts were found onboard at least two of their craft. In our opinion, these officials deserve whatever harmful actions may have been taken against them by these creatures as a result of establishing a 'relationship' with what was a malevolent alien race for mostly selfish motives. It is not certain whether this particular alien was one of the mantis-like "Infernals" or one of the reptilian "Sauroids" who apparently are subject to them. However, the movie 'CLOSE ENCOUNTERS OF THE THIRD KIND,' which whitewashed the actual malevolent nature of the aliens to an incredible degree, depicted BOTH the small saurian 'gray' type beings and the long-armed 'mantis' like creatures as working together. As we've said it seems that the desire of the secret government to obtain the occult-technology of these particular 'aliens' was one of their main motivations for establishing a WORKING contact with the saurian grays instead of with the more benevolent though protective human-alien races, even if it meant-- as we shall soon see--the sellout of their fellow humans beings to obtain this. This 'forbidden fruit' of super-technology would apparently allow the recipients to live like 'gods' over the rest of humanity - Branton).*

Kwadwo Naya: Baa Ankh Em Ra A'lyun Eil

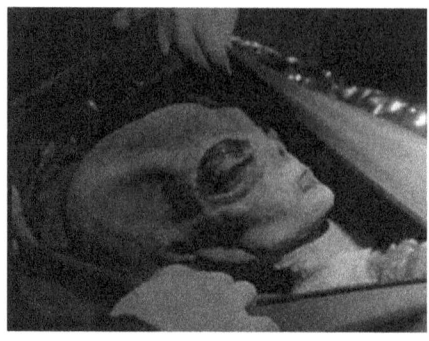

President Truman created the supersecret National Security Agency (NSA) by secret Executive order on November 4, 1952. Its primary purpose was to decipher the alien communications, language, and establish a dialogue with the extra-terrestrials. The most urgent task was a continuation of the earlier effort. The secondary purpose of the NSA was to monitor all communications and emissions from all electronic devices worldwide to gather intelligence, both human and alien, AND TO CONTAIN THE SECRET OF THE ALIEN PRESENCE. Project SIGMA was successful.

"The NSA also MAINTAINS COMMUNICATIONS WITH THE LUNA BASE AND OTHER SECRET SPACE PROGRAMS (Note: Val Valerian was sent a document which was allegedly a crew roster for 'Starfleet International U.S.S. Concord NCC-1989' which listed several military personnel and their ACTUAL service numbers. A U.S.S. Excalibur was also mentioned, piloted by WO4. Chuck Graham SFMC-8906-0001; CPL. Chuck Fair SCMC-8908- 0005; CPL. Jon Plant SCMC- 8908-0007; and WO3 Mike Wier - no service number given. Branton). By executive order of the President, the NSA is exempt from all laws which do not specifically name the NSA in the text of the law as being subject to that law. That means that if the agency is not spelled out in the text on any and every

law passed by Congress it is not subject to that or those laws. The NSA now performs many other duties and in fact, is the premier agency within the intelligence network. Today the NSA receives approximately 75 percent of the monies allotted to the intelligence community. The old saying 'where the money goes therein the power resides' is true. The DCI today is a figurehead maintained as a public ruse. The primary task of the NSA is still alien communications but now includes other extra-terrestrial projects as well.

President Truman had been keeping our allies, including the Soviet Union, informed of the developing alien problem. THIS HAD BEEN DONE IN CASE THE ALIENS TURNED OUT TO BE A THREAT TO THE HUMAN RACE (Note: Could this explain the sudden and unexpected 'fall' of the Soviet Union and 'Communism'? Although Communism still resides to a large extent in China and elsewhere its power has been greatly diminished in the Bolshevik states. The resulting international cooperation may be a two-edged sword, being either good or bad depending on how it is used. For instance, a global system might involve INDUSTRIAL cooperation which could strengthen the planet against an alien threat on the one hand while still allowing nations to retain their political independence and cultural diversities; or on the other hand, it could involve POLITICAL cooperation which may very well lead to absolute dictatorial control of the world by a person or small group of persons, which would be devastating to the "cultural diversities" which add variety to the human race, who would no doubt be *pressured give up their cultural characteristics in order to "conform" to the one-world political "beast" - Branton).*

PLANS WERE FORMULATED TO DEFEND THE EARTH IN CASE OF INVASION. Great difficulty was encountered in maintaining international secrecy. It was decided that an outside group was necessary to coordinate and control international efforts in order to hide the secret from the normal scrutiny of governments by the press. The result was the formation of a secret ruling body which became known as the Bilderberger Group. The group was formed and met for the first time in 1952. They were named after the first publicly known meeting place, the Bilderberg Hotel. That public meeting took place in 1954. They were nicknamed the Bilderbergers. The headquarters of this group is Geneva, Switzerland. The Bilderbergers evolved into a secret world government that now controls everything. The United Nations was then, and is now, an international joke.

Beginning in 1953 a new president occupied the White House. He was a man used to a structured staff organization with a chain of command. His method was to delegate authority and rule by committee. He made his decisions, but only when his advisors were unable to come up with a consensus. His normal method was to read through or listen to several alternatives and then approve one. Those who worked closely with him have stated that his favorite comment was, 'Just do whatever it takes.' He spent a lot of time on the golf course. This was not unusual for a man who had been career Army with the ultimate position of Supreme Allied Commander during the war, a post which had earned him five stars. The President was General of the Army Dwight David Eisenhower.

During his first year in office, 1953, at least 10 more crashed discs were recovered along with 26 dead and 4 live aliens. Of the 10, 4 were found in Arizona, 2 in Texas, 1 in New Mexico, 1 in Louisiana, 1 in Montana, and 1 in South Africa. There were hundreds of sightings.

Eisenhower knew that he had to wrestle and beat the alien problem. He knew that he could not do it by revealing the secret to Congress. Early in 1953, the new President turned to his friend and fellow member of the Council on Foreign Relations Nelson Rockefeller. EISENHOWER AND ROCKEFELLER BEGAN PLANNING THE SECRET STRUCTURE OF THE ALIEN-TASK SUPERVISION, which became a reality within one year. The idea for MJ-12 was thus born.

It was Nelson's uncle Winthrop Aldrich who had been crucial in convincing Eisenhower to run for President. The whole Rockefeller family and with them, the Rockefeller empire, had solidly backed Ike. Eisenhower belonged heart and soul to the Council on Foreign Relations and the Rockefeller family. ASKING ROCKEFELLER FOR HELP WITH THE ALIEN PROBLEM WAS TO BE THE BIGGEST MISTAKE EISENHOWER EVER MADE FOR THE FUTURE OF THE UNITED STATES AND MAYBE FOR HUMANITY.

Within a week of Eisenhower's election, he had appointed Nelson Rockefeller chairman of a Presidential Advisory Committee on Government Organization. Rockefeller was responsible for planning the reorganization of government, something he had dreamed of for many years. New Deal programs went into one single cabinet position called the Department of Health, Education, and Welfare. When the Congress approved the new Cabinet position in April 1953,

Nelson was named to the post of Undersecretary to Oveta Culp Hobby.

In 1953 astronomers discovered large objects in space that were tracked moving toward the Earth. It was first believed that they were asteroids. Later evidence proved that the objects could only be spaceships (perhaps hollowed-out asteroids from the asteroid field between Mars and Jupiter? - Branton). Project SIGMA intercepted alien radio communications. When the objects reached the Earth, they took up very high geosynchronous orbit around the equator. There were several huge ships, and their actual intent was unknown. Project SIGMA and a new project, PLATO, through radio communications using the computer binary language, were able to arrange a landing that resulted in face-to-face contact with alien beings from another planet. The landing took place in the desert. The movie, 'CLOSE ENCOUNTERS OF THE THIRD KIND' is a fictionalized version of the actual event. Project PLATO was tasked with establishing diplomatic relations with this race of space aliens. A hostage was left with us as a pledge that they would return and formalize a treaty.

In the meantime, a race of humanoid (Nordic-Blond? - Branton) aliens landed at Homestead Air Force Base in Florida and successfully communicated with the U.S. government. THIS GROUP WARNED US AGAINST THE RACE ORBITING THE EQUATOR AND OFFERED TO HELP US WITH OUR SPIRITUAL DEVELOPMENT. THEY DEMANDED THAT WE DISMANTLE AND DESTROY OUR NUCLEAR WEAPONS AS THE MAJOR CONDITION.

THEY REFUSED TO EXCHANGE TECHNOLOGY CITING THAT WE WERE SPIRITUALLY UNABLE TO HANDLE THE TECHNOLOGY WE ALREADY POSSESSED. THESE OVERTURES WERE REJECTED on the grounds that it would be foolish to disarm in the face of such an uncertain future. There was no track record to read from. IT MAY HAVE BEEN AN UNFORTUNATE DECISION.

The third landing at Muroc, now Edwards Air Force Base, took place in 1954. The base was closed for three days and no one was allowed to enter or leave during that time. The historical event had been planned in advance. Details of a treaty had been agreed upon. Eisenhower arranged to be in Palm Springs on vacation. On the appointed day the President was spirited to the base. The excuse was given to the press that he was visiting a dentist. Witnesses to the event have stated that three UFOs flew over the base and then landed. Antiaircraft batteries were undergoing live-fire training and the startled personnel actually fired at the crafts as they passed overhead... the shells missed and no one was injured (Note: These three crafts were apparently from the orbiting "gray" craft that the 'humanoids' warned the government about. This 'meeting' apparently resulted in one of the major 'U.S. government - Gray' treaties. The fact that the startled gunners failed to destroy the alien ships may have been unfortunate, as such an event might have led to an abort of the so-called 'treaty' deal with the grays - Branton).

President Eisenhower met with the aliens on February 20, 1954, and a formal treaty between the alien nation and the United States of America was signed. We then received our first alien ambassador from outer space. He was the hostage that had been left at the first landing in the desert. His name was

'His Omnipotent Highness Crilll or Krilll,' pronounced Crill or Krill. In the American tradition of disdain for royal titles he was secretly called 'ORIGINAL HOSTAGE CRILL, OR KRILL.' Shortly after this meeting, President Eisenhower suffered a heart attack (the judgment of God?).

Four others present at the meeting were Franklin Allen of the HEARST NEWSPAPERS, Edwin Nourse of BROOKINGS INSTITUTE, Gerald Light of METAPHYSICAL RESEARCH fame, and CATHOLIC BISHOP MacIntyre of Los Angeles. Their reaction was judged as a microcosm of what the public reaction might be. Based on this reaction, it was decided that the public could not be told. Later studies confirmed the decision as sound.

An emotionally revealing letter written by Gerald Light spells out in chilling detail: 'My dear friends: I have just returned from Muroc. The report is true -- devastatingly true! I made the journey in company with Franklin Allen of the Hearst papers and Edwin Nourse of Brookings Institute (Truman's erstwhile financial advisor) and Bishop MacIntyre of L.A. (confidential names for the present, please). When we were allowed to enter the restricted section (after about six hours in which we were checked on every possible item, event, incident, and aspect of our personal and public lives), I HAD THE DISTINCT FEELING THAT THE WORLD HAD COME TO AN END WITH FANTASTIC REALISM. FOR I HAVE NEVER SEEN SO MANY HUMAN BEINGS IN A STATE OF COMPLETE COLLAPSE AND CONFUSION, AS THEY REALIZED THAT THEIR OWN WORLD HAD INDEED ENDED WITH SUCH FINALITY AS TO BEGGAR DESCRIPTION. THE REALITY OF 'OTHER-PLANE' AEROFORMS IS NOW AND FOREVER REMOVED FROM

THE REALMS OF SPECULATION AND MADE A RATHER PAINFUL PART OF THE CONSCIOUSNESS OF EVERY RESPONSIBLE SCIENTIFIC AND POLITICAL GROUP. *During my two day visit, I saw five separate and distinct types of aircraft being studied and handled by our Air Force officials -- with the assistance and permission of the Etherians!*

I have no words to express my reactions. It has finally happened. It is now a matter of history. President Eisenhower, as you may already know, was spirited over to Muroc one night during his visit to Palm Springs recently. And it is my conviction that he will ignore the terrific conflict between the various 'authorities' and go directly to the people via radio and television -- if the impasse continues much longer. FROM WHAT I COULD GATHER, AN OFFICIAL STATEMENT TO THE COUNTRY IS BEING PREPARED FOR DELIVERY ABOUT THE MIDDLE OF MAY.'

We know that no such announcement was ever made. The silence-control group won that day. We also know that two more ships, for which we can find no witnesses, either landed sometime after the three or were already at the base before the three landed. Gerald Light specifically states that five ships were present and were undergoing study by the Air Force. HIS METAPHYSICAL EXPERIENCE IS EVIDENT IN THAT HE CALLS THE ENTITIES 'ETHERIANS.' Gerald Light capitalized 'Etherians,' calling attention to the fact that these beings might have been viewed as gods by Mr. Light (Something which the saurian "Grays" etc., apparently wished all humans would believe, and we're sure "His Omnipotent Highness Krill" would agree - Branton).

The alien emblem was known as the 'Trilateral Insignia' and was displayed on the craft and worn on the alien uniforms. Both of those landings and the second meeting were filmed. These films exist today.

The treaty stated that the aliens would not interfere in our affairs and we would not interfere in theirs. WE WOULD KEEP THEIR PRESENCE ON EARTH A SECRET. They would furnish us with advanced technology and would help us in our technological development. They would not make any treaty with any other Earth nation. THEY COULD ABDUCT HUMANS ON A LIMITED AND PERIODIC BASIS FOR THE PURPOSE OF MEDICAL EXAMINATION AND MONITORING OF OUR DEVELOPMENT, WITH THE STIPULATION THAT THE HUMANS WOULD NOT BE HARMED, WOULD BE RETURNED TO THEIR POINT OF ABDUCTION, AND WOULD HAVE NO MEMORY OF THE EVENT, AND THAT THE ALIEN NATION WOULD FURNISH MAJESTY TWELVE WITH A LIST OF ALL HUMAN CONTACTS AND ABDUCTEES ON A REGULARLY SCHEDULED BASIS.

It was agreed that each nation would receive the ambassador of the other for as long as the treaty remained in force. It was further agreed that the alien nation and the United States would exchange 16 personnel with the purpose of learning of each other. The alien 'guests' would remain on earth. THE HUMAN 'GUESTS' WOULD TRAVEL TO THE ALIEN POINT OF ORIGIN FOR A SPECIFIED PERIOD OF TIME, then return, at which point a reverse exchange would be made. A reenactment of this event was dramatized in the movie 'CLOSE ENCOUNTERS OF THE THIRD KIND.' A tipoff to who works for whom can be determined BY THE FACT THAT

Choices 2

J. ALLEN HYNEK SERVED AS THE TECHNICAL ADVISOR FOR THE FILM. I noticed that the Top Secret report containing the official version of the truth of the alien question, entitled project GRUDGE, which I read while in the Navy, was co-authored by LT. COL. FRIEND and J. ALLEN HYNEK, WHO WAS CITED AS A CIA ASSET attached to Project GRUDGE - - Hynek, the one who debunked many legitimate UFO incidents when he functioned as the scientific member of the very public Project BLUEBOOK. Hynek is the man responsible for the infamous 'it was only swamp gas' statement.

It was agreed that bases would be constructed underground for the use of the alien nation and that two bases would be constructed for the joint use of the alien nation and the United States Government. Exchange of technology would take place in the jointly occupied bases. THESE ALIEN BASES WOULD BE CONSTRUCTED UNDER INDIAN RESERVATIONS IN THE FOUR CORNERS AREA OF UTAH, COLORADO, NEW MEXICO, AND ARIZONA, and one would be constructed in an area known as Dreamland (Note: Many sources allege that the reason the 'aliens' insisted on these underground bases beneath these particular areas was that 'they' in fact are not exclusively from other planetary bodies, but that they are originally from earth and have for centuries occupied deep cavern levels beneath the earth, and more recently beneath these areas of the southwest. The 'bases' then, which most in the government would believe are of exclusively human construction for use in 'joint' operations, would actually be 'covers' or 'fronts' for actual subterranean systems already largely under the control of this saurian race. This would explain why many human workers in these 'joint' bases have been kept highly compartmentalized; why many do not realize what's taking place in the lower levels or even that such lower

> *levels exist when other deeper-level workers allege that they do; why the 'security' increases enormously the deeper one descends into these underground bases; and why the human influence decreases and the saurian-reptoid-gray-etc. influence increases the deeper one descends into these bases - Branton)."*[38]

What are your thoughts? It is true, only a small percentage of people KNOW what is going on in this world. Less than 10% I would say. The world has been run covertly by the shadow governments and the military, who have sold US out at WILL for their own selfish purposes. Most people will read this and either dismiss it as nonsense or craziness where others will read it and do nothing. Many will not even be reading.

How times have changed. Back in the day, we were all MASONS. Now there are only a few. A few GOOD ONES! Why are people DUMMIES? Why are people SLEEPING? Why do people have RABBIT in HEADLIGHT SYNDROME? I will tell YOU. FEAR and MAGIC. It is all about SARCASM, PAIN, and FEAR, working with lower vibratory frequencies, keeping US under the SPELLS, AFRAID, and SUBMISSIVE, PASSIVE, in FEAR.

---

38 http://www.illuminati-news.com/ufos-and-aliens/html/covenant-with-death.htm Accessed January 10th, 2020 @08:48

I will show YOU how this works. Let US use Princess Diana as an example. Diana was a very popular lady who really did seem to care, she found a place in royal lineage because she was part of the family. However, her life and position became threatened as she behaved and also disclosed a lot of information to the public outside of the royal protocol. To the royals, she was becoming TROUBLESOME, in a similar way to how JFK was being TROUBLESOME. Being good to the people of this world and exposing truths. Both were killed in the name of blood, money, and power. They were killed because their visions and actions conflicted with the agendas of the CONTROLLING ELITE, who constantly require perpetual conflict to justify their existence, WE SHOULD KNOW THIS AND BE AWARE. There is NOTHING WRONG with a bit of LOGIC and REASONING!

Diana's death, like that of JFK, has all the indications of being a satanic/Luciferian sacrifice. The place and time appear to have been chosen carefully, the main aim in these rituals being to create despair and grief in the public at large to someone who engendered hope in the population. When they are wiped out in a bloody way, while still young, before their potential is achieved it seems to cause mass shock, fear, into the MINDS and HEARTS of a NATION.

LOOK at 9/11, what effect did that have in the HEARTS and MINDS of the POPULATION? Do YOU THINK that their PERCEPTIONS changed afterward? Was it for the better? I remember when people didn't lock their homes or cars and often left their belongings outside. I remember when people were not running around with guns and knives. But I suppose there was no TV in those days. LOOK at US NOW. HOW THINGS have changed. Are WE REALLY going to sit back or stay asleep SUBJECTED to this MIND CONTROL? Both Diana and JFK were speaking, disclosing, actively campaigning, and taking good action aimed at making the world a better place.

Do you mind if we stop and I ask YOU a QUESTION?

QUESTION:

Do you really think, honestly and sincerely, that our government and all of its 'nooks and crannies' will act POSITIVELY, for the GREATER WELL BEING of the PEOPLE – **US** rather than the personal and private agendas of their own?

ANSWER:

Probably not because the DEEP STATE/SHADOW GOVERNMENT is alive and well, virtually beyond the reach of any elected officials, armed with their military-industrial complex and its expanding influence on society. We know their agendas, SEX, POWER, MONEY, CONTROL, and GREED. You only have to LOOK backward and forwards in history and ONE can SEE what is going on. ONE only has to FOLLOW the money. If it happens to disrupt the FLOW of MONEY one could easily get ERASED, DEFAMED, DISGRACED, IMPRISONED, or ABUSED. What happened to Diana and JFK could easily happen again, IF WE LET IT!

To them, no one is too big and small for this treatment. But WHO ARE THEY? Exactly! Despite ALL, WE have nothing to worry about, WE NEED to stop giving them our POWER and CONSENT. It is really that simple. Everything in this LIFE boils down to one of two things in the EYES of the ADMINISTRATION of the PLAN-E.T.

These things are:

LAW and COMMERCE.

This is the same stem which runs on other planets:

LAW and COMMERCE.

How much do you KNOW about INTERNATIONAL LAW? What do you KNOW about COMMERCE and the UCC codes? What is YOUR STANDING IN LAW? What is YOUR STANDING IN COMMERCE? If you are not aware of these things I suggest you find out.

LIFE is ABOUT LAW, COMMERCE, CONTRACTS, and DISCLOSURE. How many times have you read the terms on conditions on the contracts that are put in front of YOU? There is a contract behind almost everything WE TOUCH, behind literally everything WE sign, WE need to be careful when giving our signature away. What is it that WE are signing. Did my mother and father know that she was registering me as dead at sea, signing my soul over to the Vatican? Was this disclosed to them? This was a hidden contract; the facts were hidden in plain sight but my parents could not SEE enough to SEE it. Just like most of US ALL. But TIMES have CHANGED now, and WE do not need to have these tricks played on US again.

I could go on forever about DISCLOSURE, detailing the REASON WHY WE as the people are told so little. The REASON why WE, the people, are at LEAST thirty years behind is because of the information that the government passes on to US. DO you THINK if NASA FOUND ALIENS

TODAY that they would let us know? Do YOU THINK that WE would SEE it on the NEWS? No, never in a month of Sundays. We would get a bit of soft disclosure when their hands are forced but that is it. Watch out for NIBIRU, LOOK OUT for THE SHAMS, work on YOUR RIGHTEOUSNESS, and get into the RIGHT TIME (NATURAL TIME), that is all I have to say.

YOU may THINK and FEEL that I AM crazy, that is FINE, maybe I AM? Maybe YOU ARE THINKING and FEELING in YOUR SLEEP?

Here it is in a nutshell, with LOGIC and SOUND RIGHT REASONING: the people who have been running things have been misinforming and deceiving the public for well over four hundred years, they have the cooperation of the military and a lot of money at their disposal. Generally, what has been "officially" said through the media is accepted by the majority of the population who are tuned into the TV, RADIO, and INTERNET.

People who go against the rhetoric are USUALLY 'taken care of' (in some way shape or form) as these wealthy people often think that they would have a lot to lose when the public suddenly wakes up and finds out that they have been deceived.

They are right in their THOUGHTS. QUITE FRANKLY I would never want to be in their position. The POLES are GOING to REVERSE again, MARK my WORDS. A CHANGE OF GUARD IS REQUIRED! A CHANGE OF GUARD IS COMING!

This was prophesied in the bible which was written so long ago. It was prophesized once again by Malachi Z. York back in 1970, where he was saying that it would happen around the year 2030. I do not believe that these two SOURCES are wrong. There are many, many more SOURCES which have all been saying the same thing.

THE TIME IS NOW. So many people are LOOKING for answers now there is so much DISINFORMATION, but this is just a part of the GAME as YOU can IMAGINE. Do not be TRICKED! Always LOOK at the INTENTIONS and MOTIVES of the ENTITIES that YOU are dealing with and always FOLLOW the MONEY, it will help YOU BECOME more AWARE of WHAT YOU ARE DEALING WITH. OUR PLAN-E.T. needs CHANGE! WE need CHANGE! NATURE needs CHANGE.

The DEVIL and its AGENTS have been CAUSING HAVOC FOR TOO LONG. PLEASE GO AWAY!!! WE do not need YOU ANYMORE. We would like a CHANGE from POLLUTION! We would like a CHANGE from WAR! We would like a CHANGE from the PHARMACEUTICAL companies REPLACING NATURE for a PROFIT over OUR LIVES! WE would like a CHANGE from water being STOLEN from US, repackaged into bottles and sold back to US (can you IMAGINE this?). PEOPLE need to be FREE to SPEAK and TRAVEL as they once were! Don't worry, soon the whole world will wake up and realize that you, the wealthy ruling (so-called elite), are the ones that have been polluting our MINDS with so many extra-terrestrials and UFO nonsense, to cover up what has really been going on.

LOOK at all these 'OFFICIAL' ALIEN DISCLOSURE organizations, WHO have never disclosed anything substantial. I wonder why? YOU SEE OUR GOVERNMENTS and their HANDLERS are not interested in US or OUR SECURITY, not in any shape or form. They are only interested in their own agendas which are primarily, world dominance, control, and to keep making a profit. ETs have been trying to help us wake to a new reality for decades. If you do your due diligence and research you will KNOW.

Why was Edward Leadskalnin killed? Why was Tesla killed? Why did Valiant Thor go back to Venus? Who was he?

Where did he stay when he was here on earth? What was his message to OUR so-called CONTROLLING ELITE? Why did he go back? Why was Admiral Richard Byrd killed? What did he find? What message did he pass on and from who? Why has Malachi Z. York been incarcerated for 135 years? Why did the US government keep a town of 75,000 people a secret between 1942-1955? It was OAKRIDGE at the time the 5th largest town in TENNESSEE. Between 1942-1955 Oakridge did not exist, it did exist, but no one knew about it. You need to LOOK into the story and then YOU WILL SEE what happened.

I can go on for days about this stuff, but you should check it all out for yourself. I just wanted to highlight the reason why so many things have not been disclosed to the majority of the human race which has been causing most of us to BLINDLY LIVE a LIE. Please correct me if I am wrong in any of this, I would really appreciate. I will leave my email at the end.

CHAPTER 8
FREEDOM, HAPPINESS, AND CONSCIOUSNESS

Source: [39]

---

[39] Created by Photo angel – https://www.freepik.com

What comes next? Choices!

We all need to make them. We all need to decide on the life that we would like to live in. Would we like to live? Or would we like to do something different? Maybe, you need to reflect on this for yourself. Who knows? But to me, it's an obvious choice and we all need to make our choice wisely because this is our life.

The Earth's ecosystems are collapsing. We are at a crossroads of human civilization. The future of life on this beautiful planet will depend on the decisions we make today. Industrialism is cannibalizing the natural world, burning ancient rainforests, brutalizing environmentalists, and driving species that have evolved over millions of years into extinction. All these things were predicted a long time ago.

Are you free? Are you happy? Are you conscious? If you have answered yes to all these questions then maybe I need to take a leaf out of your book. I look around this world, look inside, outside, up and down, I look at people and also myself and I realize... not many people are really happy. Not many people are free. Not many people are conscious and aware of the running of life itself. Most are part of a system (sheeple), programmed collectives. Whatever happened to CREATIVITY and FREEDOM? Why do we not have inventors any more like Tesla and Leadskalnanin? Whatever happened to those? It appears that we humans are not CREATING anymore.

WHAT IS YOUR PURPOSE FOR THIS LIFE?

Now I am going to be a little selfish and speak about myself, I hope you don't mind. I am a genuine authorpreneur who works hard on my dream every day. I have an image in my head of a legacy that I would like to put down for my family. My life has been very hard so far and I wish to make sure that no one else in my family has to go through what I have been through. I have a purpose, a mission, a goal. I know what I want and what I am working towards. I know what skills I have to contribute to the world. On top of that, I consider myself to be conscious, aware, more than human sometimes. I know what it's like to get up in the morning, day in and day out, sweating on my own enterprises, creating, solving, learning, and growing every day, like a flower, that blossoms when the TIME is RIGHT. Do YOU know how much energy this takes? Surely this cannot be easy? But I would not CHANGE it for the world.

I could be on WELFARE BENEFITS, sit back, and have an easy life, but I would not be FREE. I would never be satisfied. I would never be fully aware of what it takes to look after oneself. The state would be looking after me so I would always be beholden to the state. If I upset the state or didn't stick to their rules then they would cancel my benefits. In this situation, I have no control over my own life as you can see, the state would be looking after me, not me looking after myself. There are too many of us living like this. In the short-term, it may be necessary, but in the long-term, it is better that we found another way, a better way.

If I had a job working for someone else things would not be much better, I wouldn't be happy, putting in all that energy servicing the dreams of another. It makes no sense. I would be happy to work with someone, collectively working on both of our dreams, that is the only way that this could work. I prefer to work on my own DREAMS. I like to IMAGINE and CREATE. I know it isn't the easiest thing in the world to live one's life this way, but I value the FREEDOM it brings to me. It is a very nice FEELING the SATISFACTION and JOY of WORKING on ONE's own desires.

As we all KNOW, this LIFE is not always ROSY. Often I experience frustrating days when business isn't going well at all, sometimes it isn't even going. On those days, I sometimes feel lonely, helpless, trapped in the very world in which I created. Many times I have not slept at night. Many times, I have wondered how it might be to give up and go to work for someone else for guaranteed money (which can be good at times), security, protection, and benefits. But I have a stubborn pride inside of me that will not let me sell out on my DREAMS, on my LEGACY, OUR LEGACY. Surely no one else in the FAMILY needs to suffer like I do just to have FREEDOM, HAPPINESS, and CONSCIOUSNESS?

I am CONSCIOUS and AWARE of what I want and where I am going, I even KNOW HOW I am going. I am HAPPY every day that I am working on my DREAMS and GOALS. It is satisfying doing something every day that I DIVINELY LOVE. As each day goes past I get CLOSER to the FREEDOM in which I DESIRE. One day I will look over my shoulder and I will be one hundred percent FREE. Until that day, I will show up every day and push my enterprises forward until my TRUTHS and FREEDOMS are REALIZED. That is my plan, what is YOURS?

Are YOU HAPPY? Are you CONSCIOUS/AWARE? Are you FREE?

People who've never started and run their own enterprises don't overstand. They don't know what the sweat, the struggle, and the vision means. They don't know the power it takes to keep doing it every day and they don't know what the joy of earning their own way means and what deeper victory means.

Some people don't understand what a FREE INDIVIDUAL is. They want a world of central planning. They feel a welter of emotions, all negative when they contemplate THE FREE INDIVIDUAL. Are you one of these people? Have you noticed society has an uncanny way of trying to make the individual into the collective?

For the free individual, "the highest work possible" doesn't involve leaving one's desires behind in order to become the abject servant of a cause. He doesn't suddenly develop an egoless and empty personality to "connect" with a goal that floats in an abstract realm. The free individual isn't shaped. He shapes. He doesn't fall on his knees and grovel to seek public acceptance. The sheeple, the herd, the masses usually operate on debt, obligation, guilt, and the pretense of admiration for idols. These are its currencies. On the other hand, the FREE INDIVIDUAL is not LOOKING to be a DEBTOR but more of a CREDITOR and SECURED PARTY.

Choices 2

The great psychological factors in any life are HAPPINESS, FREEDOM, and CONSCIOUSNESS. How HAPPY are YOU? How FREE are YOU? How CONSCIOUS and AWARE are YOU of LIFE itself? DO YOU KNOW YOURSELF (you would be surprised many people don't)? Do YOU have INDIVIDUAL FREEDOM? Do YOU have the POWER to PICK and CHOOSE your OWN OBJECTIVES in order to SURVIVE, or are you beholden to somebody else? Do YOU PROVIDE for YOUR family or are they LOOKED after by SOMEBODY or SOMETHING else? Is YOUR FAMILY HAPPY? Is YOUR FAMILY CONSCIOUS and AWARE? Is YOUR FAMILY FREE? Are the CHOICES that YOU make YOUR OWN?

I would appreciate YOUR THOUGHTS!

CHAPTER 9
RESPONSIBILITY, FREEDOM, AND CREATIVE POWER

Source: [40]

Are YOU RESPONSIBLE? Are YOU FREE? What CREATIVE POWER do YOU HAVE?

---

40 Created by Niekverlaan – https://www.pixabay.com

Most of US have responsibilities in LIFE for ourselves and others. Most of US are not FREE, this FACT often goes unnoticed as WE have been presented with an illusion of FREEDOM by the powers that be (the ones that we nominate). Most of US have CREATIVE POWER which is often UNREALIZED.

WHY IS THIS SO?

It is pretty simple when WE LOOK into things. We nominate OUR governments to represent US in a fair and just manner but they have been SUBTLY DECEIVING US.

But it is all in the name:

Govern = Control

Ment = Mind

Maybe WE are nothing but MIND CONTROLLED SHEEP whose realities are shaped by TEL-**LIE**-VISION and the M.E.D.I.A (Multi-Ethnic Destruction Agents)? Many of US rely on Google, Facebook, or Wikipedia if WE don't KNOW. A quick search will always give US some answers. But often the quality of this information is QUESTIONABLE. Who is

RESPONSIBLE for the CONTENT and WHAT ARE THEIR AGENDAS? This is what WE need to constantly ask ourselves.

Most of US ARE not FREE it is TRUE. FREE-DOM. DOM-FREE. Everything in this world is backward but most of US do not REALIZE. We live in an ERA where it has been a case of DOMINATION of the FREE. This has been going on for thousands of years with the last 400-500 years being exceptionally bad. WE have FREEDOM BILLS and RIGHTS in place but that is just an illusion. They SAY WE are FREE to TRAVEL but is that TRUE? Try going to an airport without a passport and SEE how you get on? Sometimes WE even need VISAS? Once upon a time, WE were FREE to travel as WE pleased - UNRESTRICTED.

What is going on?

They SAY that WE have FREEDOM of SPEECH. But do WE have FREEDOM after SPEECH if WE SAY the WRONG THINGS? Can YOU SEE where I am coming from?

When WE LOOK closely WE can SEE what is going on. Everything on this PLAN-E.T. revolves around two factors: LAW and COMMERCE! Most of US do not KNOW this, LEAVING US wallowing as a lower caste at the bottom of the

SYSTEM, barely making ends meet, existing but not LIVING. It is TRUE if YOU CONTROL the MIND of a HUMAN, YOU can CONTROL the BODY. Therefore if YOU CONTROL and CURATE the INFORMATION that RUNS THROUGH the WORLD, then ONE CAN EASILY RULE THE WORLD. IT IS SIMPLE! THINK ABOUT IT!

With POWER comes RESPONSIBILITY otherwise that POWER can EASILY be ABUSED. Unfortunately, the ONES REPRESENTING US have been abusing their POWER for too long. NOW IT IS TIME FOR THEM to GO. Let US call them SHADOW PEOPLE. The ONES that hardly show their faces, the ones that RULE FROM the SHADOWS, from the DARKNESS. What have these people got to hide? That WAY does not WORK, WE ALL KNOW THIS. WE ALL need to be ACCOUNTABLE for OUR ACTIONS, living for each other and by each other.

WE ALL SHOULD BE WALKING in THE LIGHT of the SUN as if ALL EYES CAN SEE US ALL of the TIME. Why should WE have to hide? The SHADOW people have not been doing their jobs properly, they have just been quietly working on their own agendas which have been one of bringing in SYSTEMS and STRUCTURES into interlocking alignment in order to CREATE larger MACHINES of CONTROL. The shadow people want CONTROL and they WANT CONFORMITY. They want LOYALISTS, SUPPORTERS, and ADHERENTS. They want FOLLOWERS, SUBMISSIVES, and SHEEP which means DEATH to the INDIVIDUAL - the FREE-THINKING-HUMAN. The individual FREE-THINKING-HUMAN wants FREEDOM, real FREEDOM.

Unfortunately in this day and age, not many people KNOW what is REAL and WHAT is NOT REAL.

"What is real? Real is merely what WE believe is real. Real is just electrical signals interpreted by our brains."
– Morpheus in The Matrix

That is the problem - BELIEVE. We should never just believe what is put in front of US – WE SHOULD KNOW! I cannot just BELIEVE something because it is the WAY that I have been TAUGHT or LED to BELIEVE. If one BE-**LIE**-VES they obviously don't KNOW, that is all I have to say.

"A belief is a poor substitute for experience."
– Tony Robbins

We are CURRENTLY LIVING under a SYSTEM which is not OPERATING how it should. This SYSTEM and its

ABUSERS are CONTRIBUTING to the EXTERMINATION of the FREE-THINKING HUMANS. REWARDING the POWERLESS, CLOWNISH, BADLY EDUCATED CONSUMERS who are DISTRACTED by EMERGING TECHNOLOGIES. With a COSY SUBMISSIVE CONTROLLED LIFE inside a STRUCTURE, EXISTING BLINDLY as nothing more than one of the lowest common denominators of SOCIETY. Like a pyramid, a few at the TOP of the CAPSTONE with all the KNOWLEDGE, RESOURCES, POWER, and CONTROL. The rest adrift at the bottom, living as the lowest common denominator - the lesser CLASS, the SHEEPLE.

I FEEL that it is TIME for US to CHANGE this NARRATIVE. I FEEL it is TIME for US to FLIP this PYRAMID:

Choices 2

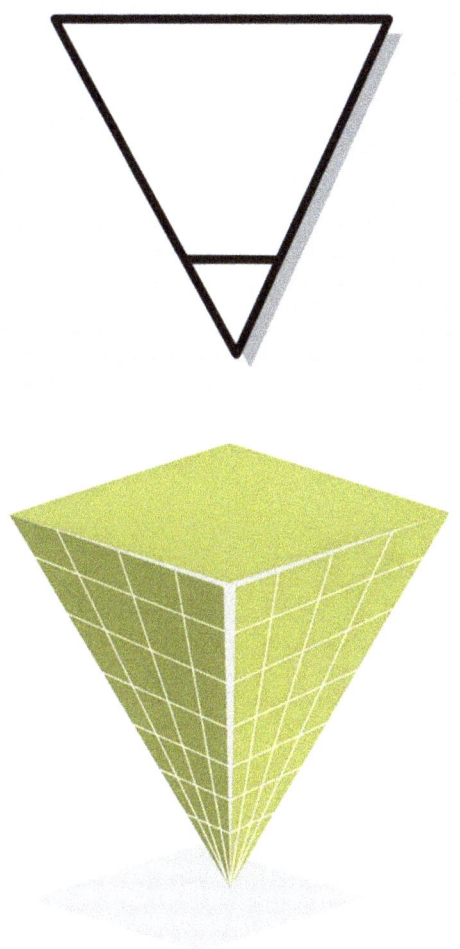

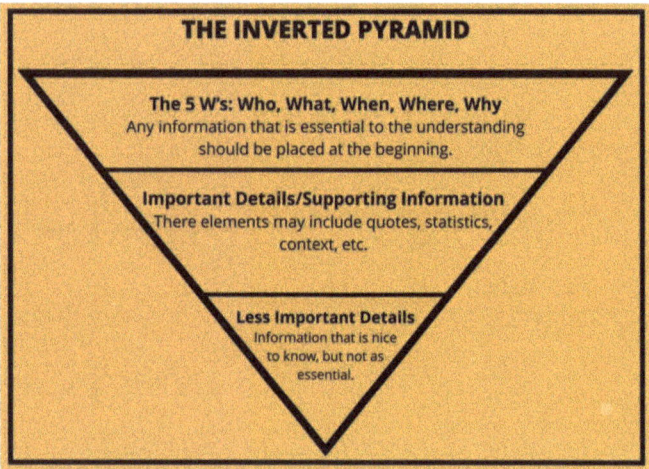

What DO YOU THINK?

Or even something like this? The TIME to CHANGE is NOW!

Many people are happy to stay doing what they are doing, that is fine. It is each to their own, I was just showing another way.

A FREE-THINKING HUMAN realizes that they want FREEDOM, REAL FREEDOM. They realize or KNOW their OWN CREATIVE POWERS. FREE-THINKING HUMANS KNOW what they WANT, they KNOW what they REALLY WANT, and they GO FOR IT. This TRANSCENDS the

MATERIAL PLANE of PERSONS, PEOPLE, and THINGS! They often SEE that OTHERS around them are not FREE. They also SEE that these people are so DEEPLY EMBEDDED in the SYSTEM LIVING under the GRAND ILLUSION of COGNITIVE DISSONANCE that they CANNOT SEE OUTSIDE of it. The IDEA of BEING FREE is MEANINGLESS to them. THEY ARE THE LOST SHEEP.

It is TIME that the PYRAMIDS of POWER and CONTROL are FLIPPED, INVERTED. I FEEL that it would be a better WAY for US to TRANSACT with ONE ANOTHER. WHAT DO YOU THINK? And HOW DO YOU FEEL?

I have left some examples for YOU to PERUSE!

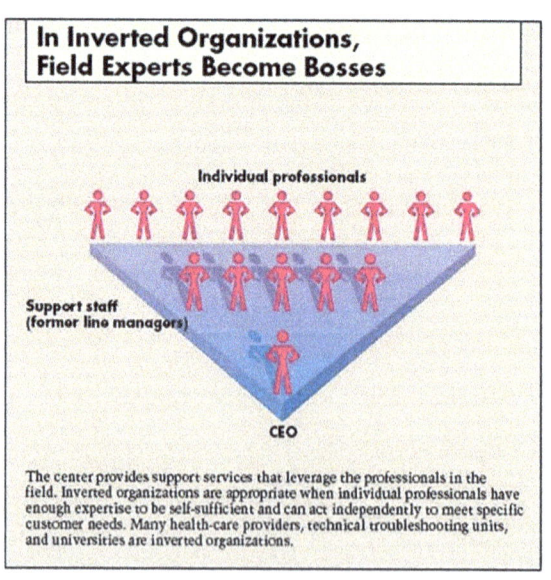

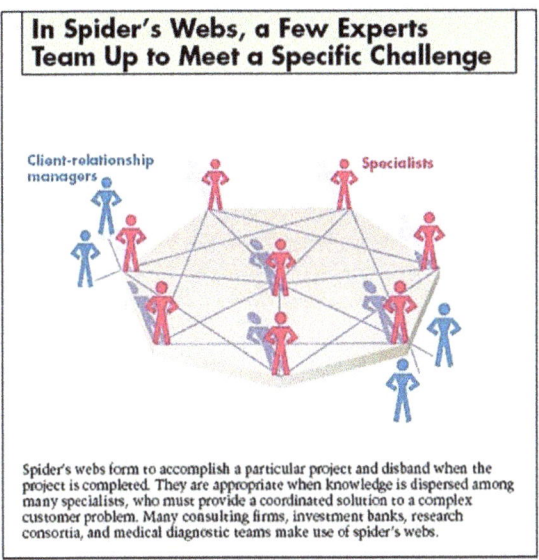

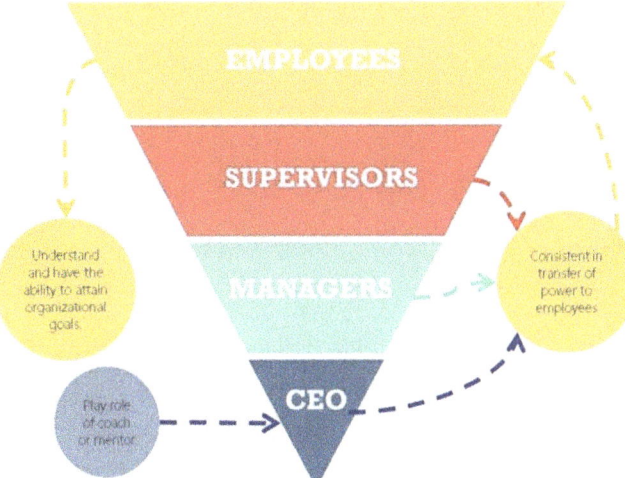

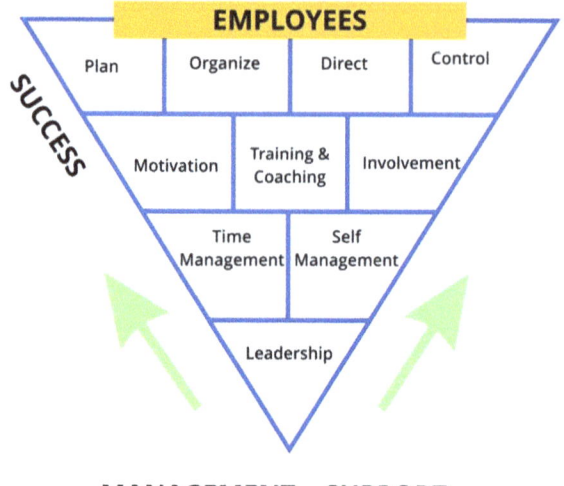

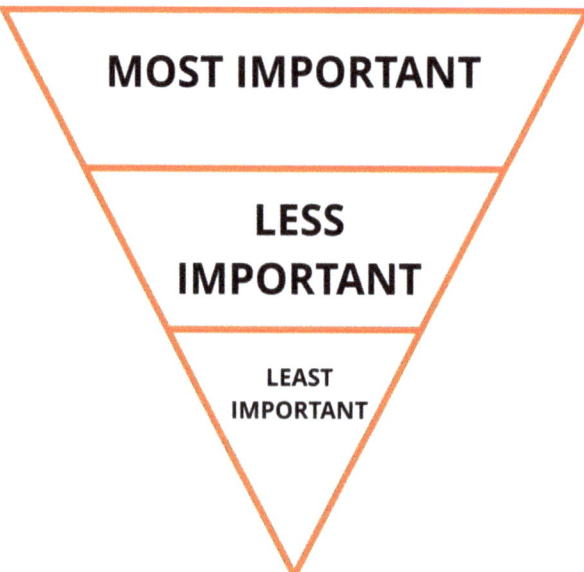

Choices 2

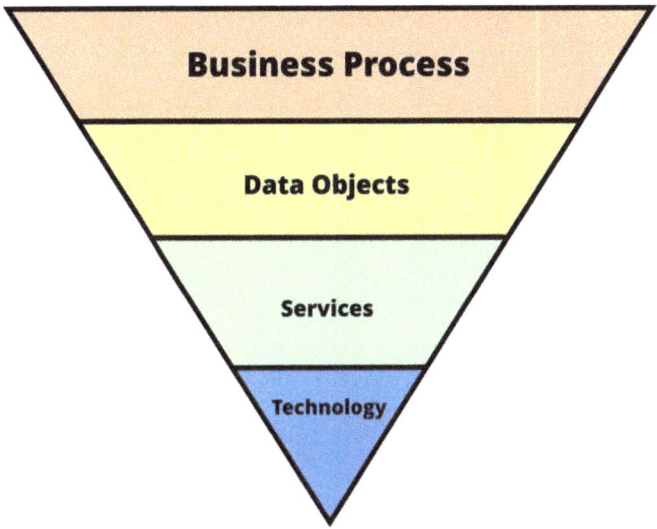

CONCLUSION

NOW is the TIME that WE all need to make CHOICES to BE FREE or NOT to BE FREE. To LIVE or to DIE? These are the questions that WE need to BE LOOKING IN TO! The CHOICES are OURS! Most of US are ENSLAVED whether WE KNOW it or not. Most of us are DEAD; DEAD in the SYSTEM, DEAD at SEA, MENTALLY DEAD.

Do you KNOW that the Vatican took over peoples' souls back in 1537 through the Convocation Papal Bull by Pope Paul III so now we're classed as cargo with no standing, which has allowed admiralty to control and dominate MOST of US since the 3rd cestui Que Vie Trust? Did YOU KNOW this? Yes, it is TRUE!

Most of US were born and delivered in a state HOSPITAL and subsequently registered for Birth. WE were then BAPTIZED but not with water and new life? A new persona was given to most of US creating joinder with other than our true biological and sanguine inheritance and right to property. Our STRAWMAN was CREATED, a FICTITIOUS ENTITY.

In the UK, all Ecclesiastical law was morphed and migrated into Civil Law before the laws of property were corrupted in the 1920s. Yet, it is openly hidden in statutes that most of US are too lazy, ignorant, or distracted to read. These people running things are very, very dark magicians who are into evil occultism. It would not surprise me if they also took blood from US at birth, hexing our blood, claiming it as their own. I have heard many people talk about the Vatican owning our souls. You may THINK that I am crazy here. The only THING I would like to say is:

AM I?

WE must give proof of life and not be attached to the state created strawman. WE must say that WE are living flesh and blood and even spill our blood. It is ALL about spiritual INCANTATIONS and REVOCATIONS. Those who KNOW, KNOW! Please correct me if I am wrong?

To cut a long story short, WE ALL need to WAKE UP and not be MIND CONTROLLED SHEEP. WE ARE NOT THE MIND and WE are NOT THE BODY, WE ARE THE ESSENCE, THE OBSERVER, THE WITNESS, THE ONE

THAT COMES BEFORE CREATION. WE ARE ALL A PART OF THE ALL AND THE ALL IS A PART OF US. WE SHOULD KNOW THIS. Many people are waiting for some DEITY to come and SAVE them when they SHOULD BE LOOKING WITHIN.

The societies that WE LIVE in are nothing but an ELUSIVE REPRESSIVE PYRAMID of MIND CONTROL. ALL is NOT as it SEEMS. Jails and prisons = BIG BUSINESS! The WHOLE SYSTEM is RIDDLED with DISHONESTY and CORRUPTION. Courts are trafficking children day in and day out under the guise of the GOOD OLD LAW. Right under our very NOSES. The CROWN PROSECUTION SERVICE administers the CENTRAL port of CONTROL in these affairs. The CPS appears to be nothing more than a well-organized child trafficking organization or a pedophile ring which includes hospitals, schools, law enforcement, orphanages, and the court system, etc.

LOOK into ALL of these THINGS and YOU WILL SEE I am sure. LOOK at all of the STUFF that has been going on in the BBC for years, LOOK at what has been happening at Walt Disney, LOOK at Jimmy Saville, Lord Epstein, and Prince Andrew. Look at the Bushes and the Clintons, I haven't even mentioned the Watergate Scandal. LOOK around YOU, YOU WILL SEE it EVERYWHERE. What I SPEAK is TRUE.

It is obvious the way they snatch children from loving homes without just cause or even correct justification or jurisdiction just to fill their agendas or desires. Children go missing from their institutions daily or suffer horrible abuse. But funnily enough, many choose to ignore it as if it is not happening, UNTIL IT HAPPENS to THEM.

What is WRONG with US SICK PEOPLE? WE MUST be UNWELL, SICK OUT OF OUR MINDS. It's time for people who love children to get proactive. What DO YOU THINK?

Read This First! Download
Why I Know That You Do Not Love Your Children!
Ebook FREE!

Just to say thanks for reading my book, I would like to give you a free e-book! ($6.99 Value)

https://BookHip.com/JFWKZB

ABOUT THE AUTHOR

Kwadw(o) Naya: Baa Ankh Em Ra A'lyun Eil

Born: Catterick Garrison, UK

Nationality: British

Race: Carbonite (Autochthonous)

Genre: Non-Fiction

Notable awards: PHD in Life and a master's in business as well as many other vocational qualifications.

Kwadw(o) Naya: Baa Ankh Em Ra A'lyun Eil is an Author, Director, Mentor and Life Coach ('Transformational'), he is a new gentleman on the scene, one of the most promising newcomers for 2019.

He was born in a country where he has never been accepted, raised in a broken poverty-stricken home, which he was thrown out at the age of 15 never to return. Surprisingly he has had a very good career, NOT GREAT, and is educated to master's level with 'degrees' in street knowledge. Despite his successes there has always been some unseen FORCES working against him, which he is only too happy to share.

Somehow, he has excelled with everything that he has touched and is not afraid of CHANGE, moving from running his own estate agency in the capital city of London (UK) to becoming a fully established author, mentor and life coach.

Kwadw(o) Naya: Baa Ankh Em Ra A'lyun Eil is ready to share his KNOWLEDGE, WISDOM, and OVERSTANDING with YOU ALL.

He has now written 21 books, and just about to finish his 22nd about COVID-19; a must read. Please watch out for it.

www.ingramcontent.com/pod-product-compliance
Lightning Source LLC
Chambersburg PA
CBHW041957080526
44588CB00021B/2773